Cincinnati's

CROSLEY FIELD

The Illustrated History of a Classic Ballpark

Cincinnati's

CROSLEY FIELD

by

Greg Rhodes

and

John Erardi

Introduction by Joe Nuxhall

Road West Publishing Company
Cincinnati, Ohio

Copyright © 1995 by Greg Rhodes and John Erardi
All rights reserved.

Road West Publishing Company
1908 Dexter Avenue
Cincinnati, Ohio 45206

ISBN 0-9641402-1-7 ◆ Third Printing

Cover by Lamson Design
Page Design by Northern Connections
Electronic Pre-Press by Berman Printing Company
Printed by Berman Printing Company

*Dedicated to the fans
who loved the old ballpark at Findlay and Western,
from the first through the gates
on Opening Day, 1912,
to the last to leave
on June 24, 1970,
and the 34 million in between,
especially our wives,
Sallie Westheimer and Barb Erardi.*

Writing this book would have been nowhere as easy nor as enjoyable without the help of many people who provided research help and shared their memories of Crosley Field. In particular, Bob Littlejohn and Richard Miller answered innumerable questions, sent us on productive research missions, and inspired us with their knowledge and affection for Crosley. Littlejohn, whose personal memories of Crosley date to the 1930s, usually has an answer to any inquiry no matter how obscure: ask him who wore number 30 for the Phillies in 1935 in the first night game, and you'll have a reply in five minutes. Richard Miller, who has collected photographs of the nation's old ballparks can often provide you not just with an answer to a question, but a delightful anecdote and a picture of proof as well.

In addition, we would like to thank John Baskin, Eric Bose, Bill Deane, John Eckberg, Bill Hugo, Ed Joost, Dick Macke, Dick Miller, Mark Rohr, John Murdough, Charles Phillips, Vada Pinson, Frank Robinson, Mike Shannon, Bernie Stowe, Gene Thompson, Jim Turner, Mark Watkins, and Howard Wilkinson for their assistance and recollections, and Chris Eckes and Kathy Bruser for their encouraging comments. Thanks also to the City of Blue Ash, especially Jenny Ramsey and Sue Bennett.

Also thanks to the many professional librarians and archivists who keep the stuff that makes books like this possible: Ray Zwick, Sally Besten, Frank Harmon, Chase Clements, Lynnette Mace, and Juanita Davis of the *Cincinnati Enquirer* library; Michael Jesse and the *Dayton Daily News* library staff; Kevin Grace of the Archives and Rare Book Department, University of Cincinnati; Gayle Renfro of the *Cincinnati Post*; Steve Gietschier and Joe Nathan of *The Sporting News* library; and Linda Bailey, Laura Chace, Barbara Dawson, Vickie Kersten, and Anne Shepherd of The Cincinnati Historical Society library.

Thanks also to Elaine Olund of Lamson Design; Roger Love and Susan DuMond of Northern Connections; and Paul Hilvert, Kristen Nelsen, Jenny Meinhardt, Chris Reed, and Nancy Roether of Berman Printing Company for their imagination and expertise.

And as always, thanks to our families and friends who have successfully endured another baseball book.

Greg Rhodes & John Erardi
March, 1995

Contents

Pre-Game

Introduction by Joe Nuxhall— The Old Lefthander Remembers Crosley Field

CROSLEY FIELD, WHAT A BALLPARK! So many of the parks back then had character: Forbes Field in Pittsburgh, Shibe Park/Connie Mack Stadium in Philadelphia, Sportsman's Park in St. Louis, Ebbetts Field in Brooklyn, and my favorite place to pitch, the Polo Grounds – if you kept the hitters away from the lines and into the gaps and center field, you were okay.

Crosley had its own idiosyncrasies: the terrace, the "Goat Run," the Sun Deck. I'd love to be able to bring it all back, but as a pitcher, I'd want it a little bigger! The "official" measurement to straightaway center was 383 feet, but we pitchers measured it at 375'. The club denied it, but we had it right there on the measuring tape. Believe me, we knew. It was a good poke down the right field line, 366', but the gap to right-center wasn't deep – 380'.

THIS BOOK BRINGS BACK SO MANY memories for me: Hooking up with the St. Louis Cardinals' Vinegar Bend Mizell on Opening Day, 1956, tied 2-2 going into the eighth. I botched a ground ball that Red Schoendienst hit up the middle. Then Stan Musial hit a two-run homer up into the Sun Deck…Beating Sandy Koufax, 2-1, in a complete game when he struck out 14, and I had 10 or 11…The great Reds players at Crosley – Gus Bell, Wally Post, Big Klu, Frank Robinson, Vada Pinson. The list goes on and on…I can still see Ewell Blackwell out on the mound, all 6-foot-6 of him. 'The Whip.' Not many hitters could stand in against him

without flinching…I can see Brooks Lawrence out there on the mound, winning 13 or 14 in a row going for Blackwell's record of 16 straight…I remember Smoky Burgess and Ed Bailey and Johnny Edwards…and 1956 – the year our club tied the home run record of 221. And, I hit two!

They added the "Goat Run" in the 1950s. They added it for Klu. They shortened the home run distance from 366' down to 340' – they thought he'd hit 10 extra homers that year – but he hit such wicked line drives, he only hit one homer into that area all year. Some guys on the other teams hit 'em there, though, like Richie Ashburn off me!

I never saw a home run hit clear over the bleachers in right field but I saw Eddie Matthews hit one off Jackie Collum to the fourth row from the top. They say Willie McCovey hit one clear over it in batting practice, but I didn't see it. The longest ball I ever saw hit at Crosley was off the bat of Ralph Kiner. There was that manufacturing building out there in straightaway center field and there was a telephone pole in front of it, at least 80 feet beyond the fence. Kiner's home run hit the transformer on the pole. That was 463' from home plate and it was still in the air.

SOME THINGS I'LL NEVER FORGET. Our clubhouse used to be on the second or third floor and we'd have to walk down the iron steps and then through the concession area. Later, when we got a new clubhouse behind third base, we'd walk through the stands. Even when they built a tunnel, there was still contact with the fans on the way out to the field and way back to the clubhouse. I liked it. You got to know people. Of course, the fans got to know you, too. Sometimes too well. I remember Duke Snider decking a fan, who apparently had gotten a little too personal.

I remember Herm Wehmeier getting ready to start a game one day in '53. One of our coaches, Earl Brucker, an old catcher in his 50's, went out to warm him up, right next to home plate in front of everybody. I don't know if Herm failed to tell him he was switching from curveballs to fastballs or what, but Herm threw a fastball and ol' Bruck had his glove down lookin' for a curve. He never got a glove on it. Hit him dead in the chest. Made a sound like when you rap your knuckles on a melon to see if it's ripe. Thump! It scared us to death. We thought Herm had killed him.

In '62 or '63, our manager, Fred Hutchinson, was really fuming after a bad loss. The players knew to stay away from Hutch at times like that. He came into the clubhouse, saw a bag of batting practice balls, and hurled 'em right through the window! There was glass flyin' and balls rollin' all over the place outside. Fans were diving on top one another trying to get the balls.

When we had time after day games, we'd go to Cliff Hase's place behind the right field wall for great roast beef sandwiches and some cold beers. There were other good places, too, behind the center field wall and on Dalton Street. They had potato pancakes, the whole bit. Unlike the players today, we didn't get fed a big spread in the clubhouse after the games. We'd be lucky to get some potato chips and dip.

One night in 1960, I pitched terrible – I had a lot of nights like that in 1960 – and I took a shower and went out to the parking lot. It was behind the visitor's clubhouse. The lot was always full of fans. I blew by everybody that night and said, "No autographs, tonight, no autographs." The next day after the game a fan named "Pops" came up to me. I knew him well. I liked him and respected him. He said, "I saw what you did last night, Joe. That's not you. That's not the kind of person you are." I've never forgotten that. Since then, I've always stopped to sign. I've always remembered what Pops told me.

THERE WERE SO MANY GREAT PROMOTIONS and entertainment acts for the fans. Between games of Sunday doubleheaders, Smitty's Band would march out behind second base and start playing…Ronnie Dale would play for 15-20 minutes after the game and people would sit there and listen…Shriner's Night was huge. Fans absolutely packed the place. The band and circus animals had the field for an hour.

I remember guys dropping baseballs from helicopters at 500 feet and players trying to catch 'em. Only one I ever saw do it was Hobie Landrith. He won $500. That was a good piece of change!

Andy Varipapa, the pro bowler, would set up two alleys near the dugout along the third-base line and do trick shots – throw two balls at once and have 'em cross alleys and get strikes, bounce balls out of the gutters for strikes…The clown princes Max Patkin and Al Schacht would come in, but the best of 'em all was Jackie Price. He'd catch baseballs hanging onto the back of a Jeep; you'd throw him four balls in rapid succession and he'd catch 'em all in the pocket of his shirt; he'd stand on his head on the mound and play catch with you…I remember the time they brought in a model-airplane guy. He had his gas planes diving and doing all kinds of stuff. He was buzzing the scoreboard with 'em, but he didn't get one of 'em up quick enough and whammm! Oh, man, I mean he smoked it. That plane broke into about 400 pieces.

WE COULD PACK 30,000 FANS INTO OLD CROSLEY. Could you imagine another Crosley Field for the city of Cincinnati? A new Crosley would seat 42,000 or 44,000. It could be built with the same design. It would strike a nostalgic chord with the fans who saw games at Crosley. The new fans would love it, too, because Crosley was so intimate. How I miss that park!

Okay, enough of me. Slide into your favorite easy chair, sit back and relax. You're about to go on a wonderful trip down Memory Lane. Before you know it, you'll be rounding third and heading for home.

The Old Lefthander
Joe Nuxhall
Plant City, Florida

More Than a Ballgame

"Peanut" Jim Shelton set up his push-cart peanut stand outside Crosley Field for 40 years, and in his top hat and bow tie became a Crosley institution.

G OING TO CROSLEY FIELD WAS ALWAYS MORE THAN JUST GOING TO A ballgame. Years later, as the the details of the games have faded, the memories of *going to Crosley* have survived.

Crosley Field won no architectural awards. It was a plain, utilitarian structure that fit comfortably into its brick and smokestack surroundings. For most of its life the traffic jams and parking nightmares were legendary, and the neighborhood around it was deteriorating. But inside, on the green grass and brown dirt, the players in their red and white uniforms made magic.

Paul Sommerkamp, who walked to Crosley as a kid from his home in Northern Kentucky, and who later became the field announcer, remembered, "There it sat, in kind of a dilapidated neighborhood, like a jewel. It was sort of an oasis. You'd walk up through the portals to the seats; the sight of that bright-green grass would hit you, and you'd think you'd walked into another world."

Crosley's dimensions were pure West End. The left field wall was York Street; center field and right field were Western Avenue; and Findlay Street bordered the right field line. The angle of Western Avenue gave the park its odd dimensions with right field always far deeper than left. Sitting in the stands, the factories beyond the parks loomed above the fence, and for a big game the windows of those buildings filled with faces. It was hard to tell where the ballpark ended and the neighborhood began.

In the 1960s, the city demolished much of the neighborhood for parking and a new interstate highway behind the outfield wall. But even that jarring intrusion could not destroy the magic of the ballpark. Frank Bitzer remembered when his father drove a truck past Crosley Field on I-75, and he went along.

"My pop died when I was ten years old. One of my fondest memories of him is sitting in that big truck and driving past Crosley Field, looking over the outfield wall and seeing the game and the crowd, and listening to my Pop tell stories about how he went to Crosley when he a kid. I really miss those days!"

Before the 1950s, Crosley Field was a streetcar park. Ted McGoron remembered: "My mother would give me 10 cents for the streetcar, 10 cents for peanuts, and 10 cents for lemonade. And things couldn't get any better than that."

If you were headed to the right field bleachers, the ticket window was on Western Avenue (just to the right of the "Home of the Reds" sign below in this photograph from the 1930s), but if you wanted grandstand seats, you walked down Findlay Street (just out of view on the far left) to the main ticket windows. Sell outs were rare in the Crosley era, and you could almost always buy a good seat. And if you had to buy standing-room-only, you could rent a milk box to stand on for a quarter.

Going to Crosley was a chance for autographs, for the players were more accessible then. They would sign their names before the games, and if you knew where to go afterwards, in back of the stands by the players' entrance, you could see your heroes in street clothes and grab one last autograph before they caught a cab for the hotels downtown.

Terry Newhard remembered taking a long train trip to Cincinnati in the 1950s to see his favorite player, Ted Kluszewski.

"I was 12 years old with a Little League troop from Fort Wayne. We rode the train down to Union Terminal and all us kids – there must have been 500 of us – walked to Crosley. I remember my mother complaining about the $12 I think it cost for the train ticket and the game ticket, but it was worth it! I saw Snider and Reese and Campanella and of course Kluszewski. After the game we walked back to the station and went home that night."

Going to the game was the fans, especially the boisterous rooters that occupied the right-field bleachers, or the Sun Deck as it came to be known (and the Moon Deck for night games).

There was never a fan like Henry Thobe (right), a bricklayer from Oxford, Ohio, whose game uniform consisted of a white suit, red tie, megaphone, and umbrella. He became such an institution that he had the run of the field, and led the cheers for the Reds from all over the park.

When he died just before Opening Day in 1950, the headlines declared "Reds Lose Greatest Fan."

Going to Crosley was Opening Day and the Findlay Market parade, and sitting in the temporary seats on the outfield terrace.

Grandparents suddenly and unexpectedly "passed away" on the eve of Opening Days or other big games. The owners of a Clifton barber shop suffered more than most, judging by a well-worn sign that frequently appeared in their window: "Gone to the Funeral at Western and Findlay Ave. Grandma Died Again. Bob and Art."

Special promotions filled the Crosley schedule, including regular Ladies Days and doubleheaders and Knothole Days. The Knotholers had their reserved sections, usually down in the right field or left field grandstands and their chant, "We wanta hit, we wanta hit," accompanied by the rhythmic clomping of feet echoed through the ballpark and became one of the lost sounds of old Crosley Field.

Going to Crosley was knowing the landmarks, and none was more famous, or infamous, than the left field terrace. It appeared benign from the stands, but pity the poor visiting outfielder unfamiliar with its steep rise.

Beyond the terrace was the laundry, more specifically the Superior Towel and Linen Service. Mention the laundry and everyone knew what you meant. It was one of the most recognizable landmarks in all of baseball. At home, listening to

Waite Hoyt call another home run into "Burgerville," when Waite said the ball hit the roof of the laundry, you knew it had gone a long way.

Crosley was red hots and bratwurst, and lemonade, soft drinks, and beer. In the stands, the beer vendors hawked local brews, including Burger and Hudepohl. And, along with the noises of the game came the calls of "Rock 'n roll with Hudepohl," and "Get moody with Hudy."

Beneath the stands, you waited out rain delays, and if you were David Hadley and his friends, you didn't care.

"In 1962, there were five of us in high school that came to Crosley from Richmond, Indiana in my '61 Valiant for every Sunday doubleheader. I think gas was 29 cents a gallon and grandstand tickets were two bucks. One drizzly Sunday, we got there about 11 o'clock for batting practice. There was a rain delay; the first game went extra innings. Then there was another rain delay between games, and both games were high-scoring. I don't think the second game started 'till 7 o'clock. We didn't leave the ballpark until 11 p.m. Twelve hours! And, you know, there was *never* any thought of leaving early. I think we got home about one in the morning, got up and went to school the next day."

Crosley Field

Going to Crosley Field was the sounds of the ballpark, of Ronnie Dale's organ music, of familiar PA voices from Harry Hartman in the 1930s to Paul Sommerkamp in the '50s and '60s, and (below) Marian Spelman stepping to the microphone and singing "The Star Spangled Banner," and the cheers of the crowd shouting, "Play Ball!" ◆

The Second

1884-1911:
Wooden Stands and a Palace

F ROM 1869, WHEN THE CINCINNATI BASE BALL CLUB INAUGURATED professional baseball, until 1883, the Reds played on three ballfields, all located in the flood plain of the Millcreek Valley on the city's west side.

The number of parks and the location made sense for the time. Baseball had not yet established a solid financial base in Cincinnati and squabbles at the national level over the economic structure of baseball led the various owners of the Reds to move cautiously, building their parks on the cheap, if not always desirable land along the Millcreek, and erecting small wooden grandstands and flimsy fences that reflected baseball's still uncertain hold on the local populace.

And so, in the winter of 1883, when the Cincinnati Base Ball Club announced plans to build a new park at the corner of Findlay Street and Western Avenue, it is unlikely that anyone foresaw that here in this abandoned brickyard, the national pastime would flourish in Cincinnati for the next 86 seasons.

In fact, the circumstances of the building of this first park suggested it was nothing more than a temporary home for the Reds.

In the early 1880s, baseball had two major leagues, the National League and the American Association. The Cincinnati club, which had been expelled from the righteous National League in 1881 for, among other sins, selling beer to fans, had played in the American Association since 1882. The club staged its games at a small park called the Bank Street Grounds, at Bank Street and Western Avenue, a site previously used for circuses and wild west shows.

At the end of the 1883 season, hundreds of players in the American Association and the National League threatened holdouts over the new "reserve clause" in which clubs claimed lifetime rights to players, stripping the players of any mobility or bargaining power. A rival league, the Union Association, formed in eight cities, including Cincinnati, giving the Queen City two professional teams. Despite its impressive start, the UA survived only one season, but its Cincinnati legacy was the first baseball park at what would become the site of Crosley Field.

In the winter of 1883, the President of the new UA club, a former officer of the Cincinnati team, used his connections to wrest the lease to the Bank Street Grounds away from the American Association Reds. This slap in the face to the old club signalled all-out war between the two organizations, and created considerable confusion for the American Association club. Where would they play in 1884?

Up stepped businessman William P. Hulbert with a solution. Hulbert, whose loyalties belonged to the old Reds, offered a five-year lease on his 750 x 400 foot lot at the corner of Findlay Street and Western Avenue. (An adjacent lot was later purchased by club.) Some small cottages, two or three stables, a garden and a brick yard occupied the tract. Hulbert agreed to tear down all of the structures and lease the property for $2,500 a year.

The club announced the deal in December of 1883 and promised a new field and grandstand by April 1, 1884, for the start of the season.

Amazingly, given the calamitous events of the next few months, the park opened as scheduled. In mid-February, the Ohio River crested at 71 feet, an all-time high, eclipsed only by the 1937 flood. The rapidly rising Millcreek swept over the new grounds delaying the start of construction. Then in late March, the worst riot the city had ever seen, before or since, resulted in 56 deaths and the burning of the court house.

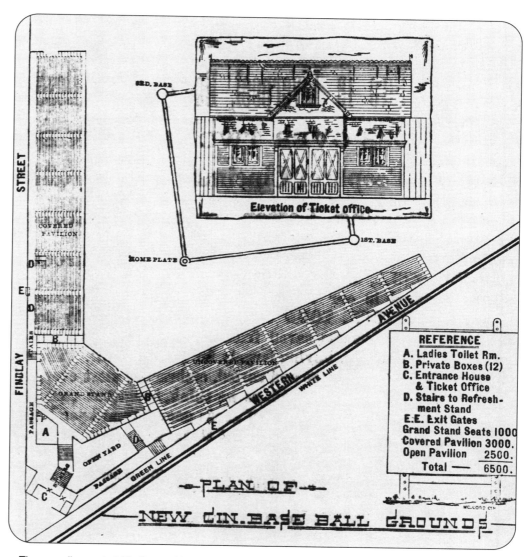

The new diamond at Findlay and Western was laid out in what was to become the right field corner of Crosley Field. Deep left field of this park was the infield of the Crosley era. On the opening day of this park in 1884, the "passage" way, parallel to Western Avenue collapsed, injuring several spectators.

It is difficult to imagine that building a new baseball park could be accomplished amidst such widespread suffering and civic upheaval, but the field was indeed ready on April 10 for an exhibition game, and for the opening of the regular season. Or so it seemed.

On a cold and damp May 1, 1884, just over 3,200 people witnessed the opening of the season and the first game at the new Cincinnati Base Ball Club Park. The contest between Cincinnati and its American Association rival Columbus, was a sloppy, high-scoring affair that featured 15 errors, and a 10-9 victory for the visitors. The game ended about 5:30 and as the fans crowded onto a small platform leading from the terrace seats to the park entrance, the wooden supports snapped and some 50 spectators tumbled 12 feet to the ground. *The Cincinnati Enquirer*, which backed the new Union Association club, claimed that 15 to 20 people were injured, with three or four "very serious injuries, one that may prove fatal." The paper ran a list of the injured fans, and a chilling account of people being nearly trampled to death in the panic and confusion.

The *Commercial Gazette*, which supported the American Association Reds, did admit that the people "who went down were badly frightened," but that their injuries were grossly over-stated by the *Enquirer*, and in fact only one fan, who had a fractured arm, "suffered any painful consequences."

The club immediately dispatched its doctor to treat the most seriously injured, and hurried to head off a public relations disaster by running an advertisement on May 3 that included statements from the builder and the architect that additional support braces had been installed and that the remaining stands were "abundantly strong enough." No future incidents occurred, and the public was forgiving; on May 3, a crowd of 4,109, almost 1,000 more than Opening Day, attended.

All the injured spectators recovered, but the initial story which predicted a fatality, has influenced authors over the years. Many books and articles report a death, but, as embarrassing to the club as the accident was, no one died.

The first grandstand ever erected at Findlay Street and Western Avenue was photographed in the early spring of 1884, after the floods of mid-February, and before the first exhibition game on April 10. The field had not yet been sodded.

One of the most unusual events at League Park during the era of the original grandstand, was the wedding at home plate on September 18, 1893, when assistant groundskeeper Louis Can married Rosie Smith. The Reds collected $60 in cash for the couple and the visiting Baltimore team coughed up another $40. The Reds, who were back in the National League, were at the end of a miserable 65-83 season, but the novelty of the wedding attracted the largest Monday crowd of the season, 2,201, including a large attendance of "ladies."

The Cincinnati Base Ball Park soon became known as League Park, and the site proved superior to the old Bank Street Grounds. When the UA club folded after the 1884 season, the Cincinnati club elected to remain in their new park.

The most significant drawbacks to the site were the placement of home plate in the southeast corner of the lot (which forced batters to look into the sun) and the lopsided shape of the field, created by the angle of Western Avenue, which produced very uneven outfield dimensions. But the streetcar lines served the site well, and some fans also appreciated the train tracks that bordered the western edge of the park. The roof of the box cars parked there provided a long-distance view of the game. On Opening Day, 1893, the *Enquirer* reported that a group of 50 men and boys were enjoying the game from this free vantage point, "when an engine backed up, hooked on and away went freight cars and spectators up Mill Creek Valley…" much to the amusement of the paying spectators inside.

Unlike a major ballpark project today, which requires years of study, financing, and construction, the original grounds at Findlay and Western were planned and built in five months, and despite fires, floods, and several remodeling projects, the Reds called this home for 86 seasons.

◆

A New Grandstand at Findlay and Western

In 1894, as the Cincinnati Reds began their 11th season of baseball at Findlay and Western, the club remodeled League Park. Club President John Brush made a major investment in the site, erecting a new iron and wood grandstand. Baseball had prospered in the early 1890s, the Findlay and Western site had proved popular, and Brush put some $12,000 in the new facility.

Not only was the grandstand new, but so was the location of home plate and the orientation of the field. Home plate, which had been located in the southeast corner of the field, was moved to the southwest corner. Now the afternoon sun would affect the right fielder instead of the batter, and the remarkable events of May 7, 1892 would not be repeated. On that date, umpire Jack Sheridan had been forced to call a game between the Reds and Boston not because of rain, or darkness, but because of *sunshine*!

In the 14th inning of a 0-0 tie, the late afternoon sun sat atop Price Hill and blinded the batters as they struggled to catch a glimpse of the ball. Sheridan deemed the situation too dangerous and called the game, a decision the *Enquirer* said may appear to be "ridiculous," but was "a just and sensible one."

Now, at the start of the 1894 season, the new horseshoe-shaped grandstand and home plate faced east; the left-field fence bordered York Street, the hills of Clifton rose above the scoreboard, and just beyond center field was Western Avenue. Except for one brief interlude in 1900-1901, this remained the orientation of the park for the next 76 years.

The capacity of the new grandstand at League Park was about 8,000, plus standing room, but a cool, blustery day held the Opening Day attendance of 1894 to just over 6,200. Gate crashers were not deterred by the cool weather. The *Enquirer* reported that before the sixth inning, a "well-dressed man" tried to climb over the fence bordering Findlay Street. An usher pushed him back over the top and the man fell 12 feet to the ground. His fall was broken however, when he landed on the back of a policeman who was peering at the game through a knothole in the fence. The newspaper reported that the policeman chased the sneak and "doled out a few 'hot wallops' with his club in a place where they would do the most good." ◆

An Opening Day newspaper cartoon from 1895 showed fans heading for the entrance of the new stands on Findlay Street.

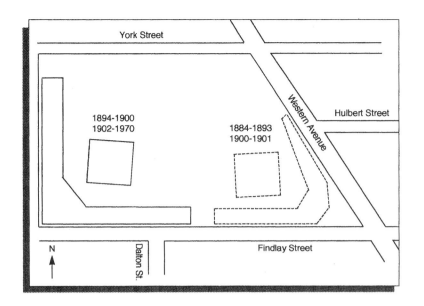

The diamond at the Findlay and Western site moved four times, alternating between the southwest and southeast corners of the lot. This map – not to scale – shows the relative position of the diamonds and the grandstands. The original diamond (1884-1893) was in the southeast corner (the "wrong" location since the sun shone in the batters' eyes); the diamond moved to the "correct" southwest corner when the new League Park grandstand opened in 1894.

When this grandstand burned in 1900, the diamond temporarily returned to the original location. Then in 1902, the diamond returned to the southwest corner when the Palace of the Fans opened and remained there all during the Redland Field and Crosley Field eras.

The 1894 renovation included the main stands, which featured three turrets topped with flags, and a covered pavilion along the right field line. Beneath the main grandstand at field level, behind a wire barricade, were two rows of field-level seats nicknamed "rooter's row."

The Times Star predicted the opening of the new grandstand would be "the greatest day in the history of baseball in Cincinnati." A cold, biting wind on April 20, 1894, held Opening Day attendance to just 6,278, but the "cranks" saw the Reds beat Chicago, 10-6.

Although this photograph is not dated, it was taken between 1894 and 1900, during the era of the turreted League Park grandstand, probably on an Opening Day. The newspapers accounts reported that the team entered League Park in decorated wagons on Opening Days.

The fans – or "cranks" – also rode to the ballpark for the annual inaugural contests, filling streetcars to overflowing and joining in impromptu parades from downtown to the ballpark. The city placed extra cars on duty to handle the crowds, which reached 15,000.

Opening Day, 1895, was marred by the death of a streetcar rider who hung from the side of an overcrowded car, brushed against a fence, and tumbled under the wheels.

The most expensive tickets to the games were the $1 box seats along the rail in the main grandstand, or "amphitheater" as it was often called (to the right in the photograph). The cranks paid 75 cents for reserved grandstand seats, 50 cents for seats in the covered pavilion to the left, and 25 cents for bleacher seats. The club also offered season tickets for $35.

Ladies were always welcome, and would normally sit in the main grandstand. The club made special arrangements for their comfort by building partitions between the pavilion and the main grandstand to spare them the stares and comments of the male cranks.

In this rare photo of game action at League Park from 1898 or 1899, the Reds batted against Pittsburgh. This photo originally appeared in a Cincinnati paper, date unknown, credited to a Maurice Lazarus of 149 West Fourth Street. The original has never been located and it is possible that Mr. Lazarus took the picture himself from the grandstand.

The game was evidently played before a capacity crowd since fans are seated along the left field fence. The caption accompanying the newspaper photo noted that the score was 1-0 in favor of Pittsburgh with the Reds in the middle of a rally. The scoreboard was visible amidst the signs in left-center field. On the mound for the Pittsburgh nine, clad in dark pants, was former Reds pitcher Billy Rhines.

When the new grandstand and fence were erected in 1894, the Enquirer reported that nearly "every foot of the big fence" was decorated in advertisements, except for a section in straight-away center field which the players requested be left unadorned so it would not interfere with their batting sight. This is standard procedure in ballparks today.

The left field signs included O. Armleder Co., advertising "Delivery Wagons, Buggies, Phaetons, Surreys, and Harness." The big hand holding a cigar touted "Hill's Utopia Cigars." Other advertisers included the John Chapman Company (bill posters), Peebles's Gold Top Champagne, Emerson Shoes, and Bellevue Beer.

Crosley Field

Fire!

Around 3:30 a.m. on May 28, 1900, the groundskeeper of the Reds, John Schwab, who lived behind the left field fence at Western Avenue and York Street, awoke to a faint orange glow and the smell of smoke. Schwab jumped into his boots, grabbed a coat, and dashed to a nearby alarm box to report that League Park was on fire.

The response by the fire department was swift, but the flames were even faster, intensified by a brisk wind and fed by the dry wood in the stands. By the time the first trucks arrived at the park, flames covered the main grandstand and the adjacent pavilion.

Along Findlay street behind the burning stands, many families in the tenement houses fled in panic from the heat and flames. Embers carried by the smoke started several small fires on the roofs of these houses, but a busy bucket brigade doused them.

Other nearby residents hastened to the scene and sat in the outfield bleachers watching the stands burn. The firemen's efforts were largely directed at saving the main ticket office and the bleachers in left and right field. Within 30 minutes, the fire was under control, but the entire main grandstand and half of the pavilion were completely destroyed. The iron pillars supporting the main grandstand lay twisted and charred. No one was hurt, although a Saint Bernard pup who belonged to third baseman Harry Steinfeldt perished.

Fire officials suspected a firebug started the blaze; other theories included a discarded cigar butt, tramps who often climbed the fence to seek shelter from the elements, and crossed wires. No firm cause was ever discovered, but ballpark fires were hardly rare in this era. Several other major league cities had experienced similar conflagrations. The Cincinnati fire was not even the first

The Cincinnati Commercial Tribune *(above) and the* Enquirer *(right), Cincinnati's leading newspapers, carried illustrations of the burned stands.*

An Enquirer *illustrator provided this view of the burned stands looking through the covered pavilion towards the main grandstand. The covered pavilion (50 cent seats) stretched along the first base line.*

This pavilion was rebuilt and when the park reopened, it became the stands along the left field line with the new location of the diamond.

The debris of the main grandstand sat in deep left field after the park reopened, which created an interesting ground rule. According to the Commercial Times*: "A batsman may take just as many bases as he can on a ball hit into the ruins."*

one at League Park. Two fires were discovered in the 1899 season in the bleachers, and a small fire was put out earlier in 1900 in the left field stands. Whatever the cause of the big fire on May 28, the club was faced with a serious problem: how could it finish the rest of the season? On June 4, the club announced it would play its next scheduled home games in mid-June on the road, move home plate to the right field corner (the site of the original diamond at League Park), and build a temporary covered stand behind the new home plate.

One month after the fire, on June 28, the new field opened. Portions of the old pavilion were rebuilt and a new grandstand behind home plate and new seats along the right field line greeted the cranks. Evidently groundskeeper Schwab could not install a grass infield in time, and the infield was left completely bare, the only skin infield in baseball.

The fire created another peculiar problem for the club and the players. In this early era of baseball, players purchased their own equipment, and when the clubhouse burned along with the stands, the Reds suffered a large personal loss of their uniforms, bats, gloves, and shoes, estimated at $1,000.

Their replacement uniforms were not ready when the club played its first game in New York after the fire. The Giants offered to loan the Reds their road uniforms, but when Cincinnati management hinted the Reds would have to pay for the replacement equipment when it arrived, the Giants rescinded the offer. They would not loan the Reds any uniforms unless the club agreed to pay the replacement costs; otherwise the Reds would be playing in their street clothes. Cincinnati management finally backed down, and agreed to foot the bill. ◆

After the fire of May 28, 1900, the Reds played the last half of the 1900 season and all the 1901 season in front of temporary grandstands erected in the southeast corner of the Findlay and Western lot. This was the location of the diamond when the park first opened in 1884.

This undated photograph showed this location, with Western Avenue running along the fence in the background. This photo was probably taken between 1884 and 1893. Note the groundskeeper's shed, the primitive scoreboard and the spectators with parasols. If this was a typical game, attendance was under 2,000.

The large building on Western Avenue behind the Strauss Tailor sign, was Hulbert Hall, erected in the mid-1880s. The building was built by the same Hulbert who originally owned the ballpark site. When the Reds lost their clubhouse in the 1900 fire, and until the new grandstand was completed in 1902, the team used the first floor of Hulbert Hall as its headquarters and locker room. Hulbert Hall, later occupied by the Oliver Schlemmer Company and the Young & Bertke Company, remained a familiar landmark until it was demolished in 1960.

Beginning in 1884, with the first season of major league baseball at League Park, through 1970 and the final game at Crosley Field, approximately 1,800 players appeared in Cincinnati uniforms at the corner of Findlay and Western.

Second baseman John Alexander "Bid" McPhee played more games than any of them.

McPhee played 18 seasons with the Reds, beginning in 1882, and from 1884 to his retirement in 1899, he appeared in an estimated 980 games at Findlay and Western. McPhee's 18-year run with Cincinnati is the second longest streak in club history. Only Dave Concepcion, at 19 seasons, played more consecutive years. When McPhee retired in 1899, he held almost all the club batting records, which were eventually broken by players named Roush, Robinson, and Rose. He still holds the club record for triples and stolen bases.

But even if McPhee never hit a lick, he would still have had a great career based on his fielding. McPhee's season marks and career records at second base are strong enough to earn him serious consideration for the Hall of Fame. Baseball historian Bill James rates McPhee as the strongest second base candidate not yet enshrined in Cooperstown.

What makes his records all the more remarkable is that McPhee accomplished most of them fielding bare-handed.

When Bid broke in, players did not wear gloves, but during the 1880s and early 1890s, most infielders began wearing soft, tight-fitting gloves, which resembled a modern batting glove more than a large padded fielding mitt. But Bid disdained the equipment. In 1890, he said, "This glove business has gone a little too far....True, hot-hit balls do sting a little at the opening of the season, but after you get used to it, there is no trouble on that score."

A sore finger at the start of the 1896 season finally forced Bid to use a glove. The result: he set a fielding average record for second basemen of .982 that lasted for 29 years.

His play drew great admiration from the fans, as did his deportment on and off the field. In an era when drunkenness plagued the game, and ejections and fights were common, McPhee played it straight. And the

McPHEE, 2d B., Cincinnati

fans loved him. When an ankle injury in 1897 threatened to end Bid's career, the fans (and even the sportswriters) held a benefit that raised $3,500.

After an unsuccessful managing stint in 1901-1902, Bid moved to the West Coast, where he scouted for the Reds until 1909. He died in 1943.

The Great Crowd

The Reds and the New York Giants battled for the league lead in the opening weeks of the 1901 season, and when the Giants visited League Park in early June, the three-game weekend series drew the largest crowds of the year. On Sunday, June 9, excursion trains brought in groups from nearby cities, including a contingent from Columbus to back Columbus native Kip Selbach, the Giants left fielder. A similar group came in from Indiana to root for their native son, pitcher Amos Rusie of the Reds.

Long before game time, thousands of local and out-of-town fans jammed the entrance to the park and the ticket office, setting off a wild dash for the unreserved seats when the gates opened.

As more and more fans arrived for the start of the game, and as all the seats filled up, business manager Frank Bancroft managed to find a bizarre assortment of temporary seats to place in foul ground between home plate and the grandstand. According to the *Enquirer*, the makeshift seats included "barber chairs, dilapidated sofas, broken down billiard tables, invalid rockers, garden settees, backless kitchen stools, carpenter's benches, and a thousand other varieties never before seen in public." Just where Bancroft pilfered these specimens was not disclosed, but the club charged 25 cents for these "seats."

Hundreds of cranks also stood in a semicircle against the fence in the outfield "packed in like sardines." Others perched on the framework of the new grandstand in left field (which would open in 1902). The roof of a large shed for construction equipment offered additional room, as did telegraph poles and rooftops outside the park. The players had to leave their benches and sit on the ground near first and third bases because of the crowds in front of the dugouts.

The enormous excitement generated by the overflow crowd did not intimidate the Giants who roared out to a 10-0 lead. Although the Reds rallied, the outcome was never in doubt and the standing-room-only crowd, bored with the game, became restless and moved closer to the infield. Fans left the stands and joined the cranks on the field, and by the late innings, fly balls were falling into the crowd for ground-rule doubles. The teams scored a total of 21 runs in the last three innings, most on account of these cheap hits. Pop fouls that would have been easy outs also fell into the crowd along the baselines and behind home plate and the fielders simply let them go.

By the ninth inning, the spectators in the outfield had moved so close to second base that routine fly balls were now sailing *over* the crowd. With the Reds at bat in the bottom of the ninth, and behind 25-13, the umpire walked to second base to try to get the crowd to retreat. Instead, he was immediately surrounded by the cranks, and he declared a forfeit.

The crowd did not object to the decision, but rather good naturedly began a melee by throwing hundreds of seat cushions. Many of the grandstand ticket holders had rented or purchased these cushions and they began tossing them at each other and at the fans on the field, who would pick them and fling them back into the stands. To add to the hilarity, one fan began ringing the bell which was used to start practice and the games.

The air was thick with flying cushions for several minutes, but no one was injured. The *Enquirer* reported that after the crowd had thinned out, "cushions were on the grand stand roof, out in the field, hanging on the fences and elsewhere." In his thick German accent, groundskeeper John Schwab said, "Dis remints me of vat a war vould be mit German pancakes for veapons." ◆

The overflow crowd created a human amphitheater around the diamond in this Enquirer illustration from June 10, 1901. Later in the game, the crowd moved so close to the infield, it caused a forfeit.

Frank Bancroft's temporary, ragamuffin seats behind home plate were not pictured, but the illustrator did include the framework of the new grandstand under construction in foul ground behind third base. This facility, eventually known as Palace of the Fans, opened at the beginning of the 1902 season, and the infield was relocated in front of the new stands. The corner from which this perspective is drawn eventually became the right field bleachers.

A Palace for the Fans

On April 17, 1902, the most distinctive grandstand ever built at a major league baseball park opened at Findlay and Western Avenue, the fabled Palace of the Fans.

There had been impressive stands erected in other cities, including Boston's South End Grounds and Baker Bowl in Philadelphia, but there had never been anything like the Palace, nor has there been since.

After the fire of 1900, owner John T. Brush hired the noted Cincinnati firm of Hake and Hake to design a new grandstand for League Park. Construction began during the 1901 season, and was completed shortly before Opening Day, 1902.

Whether the vision was Brush's or Hake's is not known, but the design produced a majestic grandstand that drew on Greek and Roman themes. What a dramatic contrast with the simple wooden parks of just 10 years earlier! Here was a baseball grandstand that could stand in proud company with the finest bank building, or school, or courthouse. Here was solid proof in concrete and iron that baseball had achieved the status not just of a pastime, but of an institution.

The main grandstand behind home plate was just the second major league stand to use concrete and iron materials. Twenty-two square columns with elaborate detailing supported the roof. The focal point of the stands was a triangular pediment that crowned a stone block with the city's name deeply etched in capital letters.

Along the front railing, gracefully curving out over the field, were 19 "fashion boxes," each divided into two sections. Behind the boxes were six rows of folding seats, and then four rows of wooden benches.

Brush and Hake knew that while the well-heeled would be attracted to the new grandstand, the beer-drinking fans would appreciate something a little less formal. Beneath the main grandstand, at field level, Brush continued the tradition he had begun with his 1894 stands: "rooter's row." Behind a wire enclosure, close to the strategically placed bars, the cranks could purchase whiskey and beer (12 glasses for a $1) and cheer or jeer the Reds, the opposition, and the umpire.

Unlike today when the construction of a new park would mean building all new stands, the photos on the following pages show that the new facility was a combination of the new main grandstand and holdover wooden stands from previous seasons. The temporary covered grandstand remained in the right field

corner, as did the covered pavilion adjacent to the main stands along the right field line. Although many baseball historians find it convenient to refer to the park between 1902 and 1911 as "The Palace of the Fans," in fact this term referred only to the new grandstand. The park itself continued to be known as League Park.

The seating capacity of the old parks was small by modern standards. For all its grandeur, the new Palace grandstand had about 3,000 seats, including the 640 denizens of "Rooter's Row;" the other wooden pavilions and bleachers may have added another 3,000. But thousands more could be admitted as standees, and such was the case on on April 17, 1902, when the Palace was unveiled.

The *Enquirer* estimated the attendance at 10,000, which included many standees in the outfield. By contrast, Opening Day, 1901, drew only 4,800.

The day began with a trolley car parade from downtown to the park, with the Reds and the visiting Cubs on board, dressed in their uniforms and waving to the crowds. Long before the game began, the stands were full, and a band entertained the pre-game crowd. The fans all rose in cheer when the teams entered the field.

Many in the crowd came from out-of-town, the *Enquirer* noting "people from no less than 50 of Cincinnati's sister cities and villages in the three states, and even as far away as West Virginia…had reserved seats in the grandstand."

Chicago won easily, 6-1, in a game marred by seven errors, which the *Times-Star* attributed to the "rough condition of the grounds and especially of the new diamond."

On May 16, 1902, the stands were formally dedicated with local and visiting dignitaries on hand; 5,000 attended and each fan received a dedication booklet. Owner John Brush invited several National League owners to the event, but only Frank Robinson of the St. Louis club attended. Brush pulled off quite a practical joke on his old friend. During the Reds-Giant game, Brush had his scoreboard operator post fake scores of the St.Louis-Brooklyn game; after six innings, Robinson's club was "trailing" 38-2. Only after the dejected Robinson return to his hotel downtown, did he learn of Brush's shenanigans. ◆

This panoramic view of the new grandstand was included in the dedication program, as were the photographs on the next two pages.

The Palace of the Fans grandstand was constructed entirely of "concrete and twisted iron" according to the dedication booklet.

The center box was reserved for club officials and visiting dignitaries. On Opening Days, the owner or the mayor would rise from his seat in this box and shout out a few remarks to commemorate the opening of another season.

In 1911, club president Gary Herrmann forever earned the admiration of the cranks when he elected to forego his speech. The Enquirer approved of the decision: "Most of the crowd can't hear it and shouts 'Play Ball,' 'Shut up,' 'Go to the hay,' etc. embarrassing the orator.... Mr. Herrmann deserves the thanks of the fans."

Right: *A bar beneath the main stands served whiskey, beer, and cigars.*

Below: *League Park in the Palace era was a mixture of old and new; the wooden stands rebuilt after the 1900 fire stretched down the right field line. The break in these stands marked the main entrance off Findlay Street. Note also the player's bench on the field. The new grandstand did not include dugouts.*

The three types of seats in the Palace were visible in this photograph: the wooden chairs for the box seats, the folding seats, and the benches in the last four rows.

The Palace of the Fans renovation to League Park in 1902 soon proved too small. Additional seats and other modifications were made between 1902 and 1911 (when the Palace was torn down). One was the extra tier of seats, an abbreviated upper deck, above the main grandstand, visible in this 1907 photograph. Note the "Y" shaped supports, a sure sign that this addition to the concrete and iron stand was built of wood.

Another improvement, visible in the photograph on page 36, was the addition of covered concrete and iron pavilions on each end of the main grandstand.

Right: *This blurry but significant photograph of League Park during the Palace era showed double-decked stands down the left field line. The club added these between 1902 and 1906 to increase capacity. A 1906 Opening Day story confirmed this wooden monster. Jack Ryder of the* Enquirer *reported that "the huge double-decker overlooking Jack Barry's territory" was jammed with fans. Barry played left field for the Reds. Cincinnati fans would not see another double-decked stand that reached the outfield wall until 1939.*

The club also improved seating in right field by extending the roof over the right field bleachers. This photograph is not dated, nor are the teams identified, but the runner's uniform appears to say "Toledo." Perhaps this was an exhibition game.

The Sausage King Takes the Throne

From a perch high atop the Palace of the Fans in 1902, new Reds president Garry Herrmann, 43, could look toward the city which included the house where he was born, the print shop where he learned his first trade, the political ward where he rose to power in the Boss Cox machine, the courthouse where he held sway, the world-class $11 million waterworks he built, and the breweries and butcher shops from which emanated the beer and sausage that made him the magnate of the moveable feast.

The $150,000 it cost to buy the club came mostly from the yeast and gin kings, Julius and Max Fleischmann, and Cox, but Herrmann put up a piece of the action and was given unfettered operation by his partners. They trusted his judgment.

Why shouldn't they?

He was charismatic, smart, and had learned the value of hard work at an early age. Garry had gone to work after just five years of school. Herrmann and his brother were orphaned when their German-born parents, Christian and Margaret Meyer, had died.

His first job was filling salt sacks. Next he became an errand boy, a printer's devil (a gofer), a printer, and then wisely involved himself in 11th ward Republican politics. It paved his way to take charge of the new, official paper of the Hamilton County Court system and ultimately opened a career of public service (assistant clerk in the police court, member of the Board of Education) and a fast friendship as Cox's trusted lieutenant who ran City Hall.

Herrmann's magnetic personality and his exuberance for living were a siren song to those around him. When he presided at a restaurant or saloon, he would start at one table, but more tables had to be added as his friends stopped by. He was the very embodiment of Cincinnati culture at the turn of the century –

evening gatherings in outdoor beer gardens, singing waiters, foaming steins of beer, ribs, sauerkraut, and guffawing laughter.

"A glass of beer never hurt anybody," Herrmann was fond of saying, " and two glasses are bound to be a big help."

He promoted Cincinnati at every turn, with its beer, sausage, and Gemutlichkeit. He brought huge national conventions to town – the Elks and the American Bowling Congress.

He was also the embodiment of class in a city not widely known for it. Impeccably dressed, moustache trimmed, hair neatly slicked, diamond rings on both fingers. He traveled in style. Riding private Pullman trains to out-of-town games, he carried along his own cargo of lager and wine, sausage and breads. It wasn't a problem until Prohibition. Federal agents swooped down on him in St. Louis, confiscated his beverages, and indicted him. Nothing came of the indictment – Herrmann was friends with fellow Ohioan, President Warren G. Harding – but thereafter Herrmann became slightly more discreet. Gastronomically, he remained unabashed: he was responsible for fried pig's feet being on the breakfast menu at New York's famous Waldorf-Astoria.

But for all his swagger and bluster, Herrmann knew baseball and his fellow owners respected him as a savvy pol who got things done. In 1903, Herrmann was elected head of baseball's National Commission – the forerunner of the Commissioner's office – and in that role he forged an agreement between the warring American and National Leagues on post-season play. In other words, the World Series.

"What's the use of our fighting each other," he asked, "when the crowd on the bleachers is yelling 'Play ball!'?"

Thereafter, he was recognized as the "Father of the World

Series," and the fall classics became like his personal presidential conventions: wild and crazy, the ultimate stage. He enjoyed every minute of it. His entourage was the largest, and best supplied, in baseball.

Herrmann's role as a mediator and public relations man in the Cox machine had served him well, and his chairmanship of the National Commission re-elevated Cincinnati to the capital of the baseball world.

But then came 1919 and the gamblers. Although Herrmann had nothing to do with the fixing of the 1919 Series or the subsequent attempted whitewash, the marvelous team which he assembled had won a tainted championship. Baseball's black eye meant the end of Herrmann's Commission.

For those who wonder why Herrmann is not in the Baseball Hall of Fame, they need look no further than 1919. Nonetheless, his legacy is secure.

"There can be no doubt," said former National League president John Heydler, "that the outstanding act of Mr. Herrmann's baseball career was the part he played in bringing the two leagues together and getting them to sign that peace agreement in Cincinnati on January 10, 1903. His work starting those peace negotiations should rank right up with the outstanding and vital events in the history of the national game."

Herrmann died in 1931 at age 71, a victim of too many sausages, ribs, pig's feet, and blood pudding. "Hardening of the arteries" was listed as the primary cause of death. Had Herrmann – and anybody else – known about the danger of cholesterol, he might have changed his lifestyle.

Then again, he probably wouldn't have changed a thing. ◆

Garry Herrmann was president of the Reds from 1902 to 1927.

"Bugs" Fill the Palace on Opening Days

In the era of the Palace, as the club had done since 1876, the Reds opened each season at home, and Opening Day had already attained the status of an unofficial holiday.

Children cut school, businessmen took the afternoon off, and according to Jack Ryder of the *Enquirer*, there was a "frightful mortality among grandmothers, aunts and cousins, which makes it imperative…that office boys and other such steady toilers should be absent from their scenes of labor…." The average attendance at Reds games during the Palace years (1902-1911) was 4,480, but Opening Day drew as many as 20,000.

There was no Findlay Market parade (that didn't begin until 1920), but there were dozens of impromptu processions that started downtown or in the neighborhoods. "They came in carriages, on Tallyhos, in chugging auto cars, on bicycles, in street cars and on foot," wrote Ryder in 1906. Tallyhos were large horse-drawn wagons decorated with banners and flags. Many clubs and organizations made their grand entrance onto the field riding through the carriage gate, the passenger all using their horns, rattlers, and other noisemakers. Extra street cars also brought thousands to the park, and after the game, 50 trolleys stood along Western Avenue and Dalton Street, waiting to empty the park.

The gregarious club president Garry Herrmann usually arrived an hour before the game and made his way through the grandstand greeting fans and friends. Herrmann was an exceptionally popular figure at the ballpark, even with his crackdown on the rowdy behavior of the "Rooter's Row" crowd beneath the grandstand. Tired of the vulgar language used by the often inebriated "bugs" (as the "cranks" had come to be known), Herrmann issued orders to his park police in 1910 to evict any spectator who verbally abused players or umpires.

Prior to game time on Opening Day, John C. Weber's Military Band entertained the crowd from chairs on the field, playing marches and popular tunes. A loud clang of a bell announced game time – usually 3:00 – and the players gathered in a semicircle in front of the main box. The mayor or another dignitary addressed the players and the crowd, then tossed out a ball to the players, and shouted "Play Ball!" ◆

Weber's Band entertained the crowd on Opening Days. The concrete and iron pavilion extension, matching the original grandstand, stretched past third base.

On Opening Day, 1908, a then-record crowd of 18,000 filled the grandstand and stood in the outfield.

If the right field stands look a long way off, they were. The dimensions of the field were enormous and very lopsided, due to the odd dimensions of the Findlay and Western lot. It was 450 feet down the right field line; 414 to right center; 387 to straight away center field; 387 to left center; and 342 down the left field line. (These estimates are based on a 1909 site map drawn by architect Hake.)

The 1900 fans loved the big new Palace field. As John Schwab, the German groundskeeper put it in an Enquirer interview, "I loaf do see dem home runts."

But Schwab wasn't talking about homers hit over the fence. The turn-of-the-century game featured big fields and inside-the-park home runs. Home runs over the fence were a rarity, and often occurred only because of the proximity of the fences to home plate due to the peculiar dimensions created by the neighborhood streets that enclosed the parks.

In the above photograph, the Cubs were at bat and the Reds in the field. Outfielder Frank "Wildfire" Schulte had just struck the first hit of the game. Pitching for the Reds was "Long" Bob Ewing and the first baseman was John Ganzel, who also managed the 1908 Reds. Catching was Cincinnati native George "Admiral" Schlei.

Another Cincinnati native on the field, and one who would have a much more distinguished career than Schlei, was second baseman Miller Huggins. Huggins played 13 years for Cincinnati and St. Louis, but then earned his Hall of Fame honors (he was inducted in 1964) as the manager of the great Yankee teams of the 1920s.

The Cubs won the opener, 4-3, and went on to capture the National League pennant and the World Series. The Reds struggled to a 73-81 record and a fifth place finish.

An Early Experiment in Night Baseball

Every long-time fan of the Reds knows that Crosley Field held the honor of hosting the first night game in Major League Baseball, in May of 1935. But there had been many demonstrations of baseball under the filaments prior to '35, as inventors and electric company boosters attempted to prove its viability.

The early demonstrations, especially those before 1900, could not produce enough light to be successful, but after the turn of the century, a Massachusetts inventor named George Cahill developed a system that earned a serious look. In 1908, Cahill persuaded club president Garry Herrmann to stage an experiment at League Park, and prior to the 1909 season opener Cahill brought his five light towers to Cincinnati.

The light towers were up by Opening Day and must have made an impressive sight. From today's perspective, however, the system seems pitiful. Cahill's five towers contained a total of only 14 lights. The arc lamps contained large carbon filaments – as large as baseball bats – that frequently burned out, and an operator stood on each tower, prepared to reload the filaments.

Cahill tested and modified the equipment and the Reds scheduled a demonstration for June 17. The early trials were not too impressive, but the *Enquirer* noted that at no time had all the lights been on simultaneously. But for the 17th, "Inventor Cahill…expects to have all 14 of the huge flaming arc lamps ready for business…."

Despite the intention to determine if the lights could be used by major league teams, two amateur clubs were picked for the game, Elks teams from Cincinnati and Newport, Kentucky. (The proceeds from the game went to Herrmann, who was a leader in the local Elks organization, and who was a candidate for Grand Exalted Ruler of the order.)

Three other major league owners attended the demonstration, which was finally held on June 18 after rain cancelled the original date. Approximately 5,000 fans attended including several members of the Reds and the Phillies who had played a game that afternoon.

The *Times-Star* claimed the field was "well flooded with light, demonstrating that night baseball is not impractical and that illumination at the park can be used to excellent advantage for all sorts of outdoor games and contests."

The paper ran the following critique of the performance of the lights on the game:

• The lights worked "fine" for pitchers and batters, who had "no trouble" seeing the ball.

• The infielders "appeared to be in a shadow," but they were able to take throws, field grounders, and catch pop flies.

• The outfielders "seemed able to follow fly balls without trouble, but were unable to get a right line on ground balls." On several occasions, the outfielders completely lost sight of the hit, and the infielders had to point out the path of the ball.

Cahill thought the demonstration could have been improved if his operators had more experience in anticipating and following the action.

Even if the test had been an overwhelming success, the major league owners were not yet prepared to embrace the concept. It would be another 26 years before lighting improvements, a change in philosophy, and a tenacious Cincinnati general manager named Larry McPhail enabled night baseball to become reality. ◆

Two Elks teams from Greater Cincinnati played in a demonstration of night baseball at Cincinnati's League Park in 1909. Inventor and promoter George Cahill had approached the Reds because Garry Herrmann, the Reds president, was also the head of baseball's ruling body, the National Commission. Herrmann had originally agreed to use major league players, but later substituted amateurs. The Reds and the Phillies, who had played that afternoon, watched from the stands. Ironically, it would be these two clubs that would oppose each other in the first major league night game in 1935.

Crosley Field

The Third

1912-1919:
Redland Rises

Prominent Cincinnati architect Henry Hake prepared the Redland plans.

AFTER THE 1911 SEASON, THE CINCINNATI BASE BALL CLUB DEMOLISHED the elegant, but inadequate Palace of the Fans grandstand and the other wooden stands at League Park, and began construction on Redland Field, the first truly modern park at the Findlay and Western site. This was the ballpark that would eventually become Crosley Field in 1934 when the club was purchased by Powel Crosley, Jr.

Unlike the Palace renovation, when a new concrete and iron grandstand was simply added to the old wooden bleachers, the new facility represented a total overhaul, at a cost of $400,000. The project sprung from a number of factors: there were too few seats, especially box seats in the Palace grandstand; the older wooden bleachers badly needed repair; and the growing popularity of baseball (inspired in part by such stars as Honus Wagner, Christy Mathewson, and Ty Cobb) had created a demand for bigger, more substantial parks.

Redland Field was built in the midst of a baseball park boom, and Cincinnati architect Harry Hake's design reflected the national trend of larger concrete and steel stands. By 1912, when Redland Field opened, three other concrete and steel parks were already operating: Shibe Park in Philadelphia, Pittsburgh's Forbes Field, and Comiskey Park in Chicago. And over the next three years, Detroit's Tiger Stadium, Fenway Park in Boston, Ebbets Field in Brooklyn, Chicago's Wrigley Field, and Braves Field in Boston all opened their doors.

The demolition of the old stands and the construction of Redland took just seven months, and much of the work was done during a winter that was rated as the worst in 40 years. And in late March, with Opening Day less than three weeks away, the nearby Millcreek rose and flooded much of the field.

Matty Schwab led the grounds crew as they swept the water and mud off the grounds. Working frantically to lay the rest of the sod in time for the grand opening, they even finished an outfield section during an exhibition game, and the field was ready for Opening Day on April 11, 1912. ◆

The concrete supports of the Palace grandstand remained standing as workers cleared away debris in this view looking towards right field and Western Avenue. Temporary railroad tracks were built to bring in supplies and haul out debris. The demolition of the old stands, including the remaining wooden bleachers from the 1890s, took just 15 days.

The construction of the new grandstand occurred during the winter of 1911-12, the hardest winter anyone could remember. In this view of Redland Field, looking west toward the left field stands from the right field bleachers, the roof over the left field pavilion was not yet installed.

Civic pride mounted along with the progress of the park: "the handsomest in the land," bragged the Times-Star; "the finest grandstand in the country," crowed the Enquirer. The grandstands and the right field bleachers seated 20,696 (this figure based on architect Hake's seating charts), and several thousand more could stand in the outfield or in the standing-room-only sections of the stands.

Construction required 800,000 pounds of steel, 12,000 barrels of cement, and 619,000 bricks. The project employed 123 carpenters, 463 laborers, 69 iron workers, 32 bricklayers, 20 hodcarriers, and numerous painters, plumbers, gasfitters, engineers, and teams of horses.

Compared to the grand Palace of the Fans, the new park was short on memorable architectural details, the exception being this wing housing the administrative offices, the ticket windows, and the Reds locker room. It occupied the far southwest corner of the grounds at the end of Findlay Street.

The unadorned, red brick exterior walls of the stands, to the right of the main offices, meshed perfectly with the neighborhood. With railroad tracks to the west, brick row houses along Findlay, and factories lining Western Avenue, the architecture of the park reflected the working class surroundings.

The Opening of the "Magnificent Baseball Resort"

For nineteen-year-old Mike Maxwell, Thursday, April 11, 1912, the Opening Day of the season and the unveiling of the new ballpark, began at 8:00 a.m. Maxwell was the first person in line for the the 25 cents unreserved bleacher seats, but he soon had company. By 11:30, when the ticket windows opened, long lines stretched along Western Avenue, and the 4,000 bleacher seats sold quickly. The gates opened at noon, three hours before game time, and Maxwell may well have been the first fan into Redland/Crosley Field.

The reserved sections of the main grandstand filled more slowly; some of the bugs were celebrating in automobile and trolley parades that started uptown or in the neighborhoods. The sunny spring-like day insured a huge turnout and the official attendance was 26,336, topping the old mark by 5,500. The seating capacity of the park was 20,696, so nearly 6,000 fans stood in the outfield and at the rear of the stands.

Most fans arrived on foot or by trolley, but over 200 automobiles filled the lot to the west of the park, and dozens more were parked along the streets. The fans came with "cameras, opera glasses and cushions; smoked bad cigars and some good ones, drank green pop, ate molasses popcorn and 'hot dogs'…," wrote the *Enquirer's* Jack Ryder.

The Reds appeared at 2 o'clock to take batting practice, and their opponents, the Chicago Cubs, wearing dark blue uniforms soon followed. At 2:30, the clubs, led by

Weber's band, marched to the flagpole in center field where, caps in hand, they watched the raising of the flag. The teams then marched back to the stands to a box on the first base side to listen to a brief address by Mayor Hunt, who after his stirring words, tossed out the first ball, and the Redland/Crosley Field era had begun.

The Cubs, who were a perennial pennant contender in this era, took a 5-0 lead, but the Reds, who regularly occupied the second division, scored six runs in the fourth inning and won, 10-6. It was only the fourth opener the Reds had won in 12 years, and everyone agreed it was just the right start for the new park. The *Times Star* reported the victory "seemed to set the Queen City wild and the downtown streets Thursday night resembled a Mardi Gras night in New Orleans." ◆

Left: *On Sunday, March 31, two weeks before Opening Day, the public was invited to inspect the new facility at Findlay and Western. A lovely spring day brought out thousands of spectators who toured the bleachers and the right field stands: a "magnificent resort" said one reporter.*

Despite being the sabbath, the grounds crew worked to finish the field.

Above: *The opening of the new baseball park merited front page coverage in a time when baseball news seldom received such prominent placement. The* Commercial Tribune's *front-page photograph showed Weber's Band (middle) leading the Reds (right) and the Cubs (left) back to the grandstand after the flag-raising ceremony. Matty Schwab's original scoreboard is visible at the far left.*

Club President Garry Herrmann was saluted for "the erection of the greatest baseball plant in the world," and the two "star" players pictured were catcher Larry McLean (left) and shortstop Jimmy Esmond.

The 26,336 spectators who filled the grandstand and stood in the outfield of the new park set a Cincinnati attendance record on April 11, 1912.

President Garry Herrmann had not yet named the new ballpark on Opening Day, and the inscription on the photo simply says "National League Park." Most fans and the newspapers wanted Herrmann to name the park after himself as other owners had done (Shibe, Forbes, Comiskey). "Herrmann Park" or "Garry Field" were popular choices, but Herrmann would not let his name be used; he favored keeping the name of "League Park."

According to the Enquirer, Herrmann changed his mind the day after the opener when the name "Redland Field" was suggested to him. The name commemorated "the famous color which has been the trade-mark of Cincinnati teams for more than 40 years." The name was officially recognized on May 18, 1912, when the field was formally dedicated.

Although the dimensions of the field were smaller than the previous Palace of the Fans park, the configuration of York Street, Western

Opening Game, Cincinnati National League Park. Cincinnati vs. Chicago

Avenue, and Findlay Street combined to create a massive playing field, the largest in the major leagues at that time. The dimensions have usually been reported as 360 feet down each foul line and 420 feet to straight away center; however, right field was always longer than left field at Redland. According to a 1911 plan of the field by architect Hake, the distance to the right field corner was 400 feet.

The bugs of 1912 loved the large field, for it led to many extra-base hits. Most parks of this era had very spacious outfields. In later years, as the influence of Babe Ruth and the over-the-fence home run became more popular, the club shortened the distances to the fences by moving home plate out some 40 feet.

Note Matty Schwab's groundskeeping artistry in the scallop swirl of the infield. The infield retained this distinctive pattern into the 1920s. Schwab also landscaped the pitcher's mound into the shape of the ace of spades for this grand opening game, but unfortunately it is not visible.

Matty Schwab: King of Diamonds

The ballparks at Findlay and Western went by many different names over the years: League Park, Palace of the Fans, Redland, Crosley. But somewhere along the way, someone should have named it "Schwab's Field," for no one knew the nooks and crannies of the old place, nor understood better how to dress it up for an important date than Mathias (Matty) C. Schwab.

Matty Schwab was the Park Superintendent of Cincinnati's ballparks for 60 years, and he learned the trade from his father for ten years before that, making it a run of seven decades, from 1894 to 1963, before he finally retired at the age of 83. Of course, there was another Schwab in line to take his place.

From Bid McPhee to Frank Robinson, from Noodles Hahn to Jim Maloney, Matty Schwab tended the grounds at Findlay and Western, and he earned such a reputation that his inventions, advice, and even relatives were sought by baseball people from coast to coast. His brother Leonard once provided the manicures for Ebbets Field, and son Matthew headed up the New York Giants crew for years.

When Matty started in the trade in 1894, the crew consisted of himself, his father, and several neighborhood kids they rounded up to help with the daily chores, and then rewarded with free seats. With Tom Sawyer flair, Matty and his father had the older kids standing in line to mow the outfield grass (with a hand-propelled mower). Matty never said whether this volunteer crew also whitewashed the fence.

As much as for his groundskeeping skills, Matty also received recognition for his scoreboard design. He described his first scoreboard, in 1894, as "just some boards against the wall." But with the opening of Redland in 1912, Matty created a clean, simple display for player's names and positions, balls and strikes, and scores of other games. We take such information for granted today, but Matty was the first to design a scoreboard to handle it all, and the other clubs soon noticed. Matty designed scoreboards for clubs in Boston, New York (Yankees and Dodgers), Pittsburgh and Philadelphia. He also invented the style of bases that strap to spikes imbedded in the ground, a style still used today.

Every year, Matty would sew new grass seed in the outfield, and every other season, he plowed up the infield to remake it. He installed a drainage system under the field, and continually modified it, as the frequent spring floods and sudden Cincinnati thunderstorms challenged his ingenuity.

Matty retired in 1963 (but not before training his grandson Mike Dolan to carry on the Schwab tradition), and died in 1970 at the age of 90. They shut down Crosley that year, too, but how could they go on after Matty? After all, it was Schwab's field. ◆

Matty's original scoreboard at Redland Field featured a bank of speakers beneath a giant Lifebuoy sign. The board measured 54 feet across by 15 feet high, and it was located at the junction of the left field and center field walls, where all subsequent scoreboards were built. Two men ran the board, with the aid of a telephone connection to the press box in the grandstand. Although some of the new scoreboards of this era featured electric bulbs, Matty simply used very large numbers.

The numbers at the bottom of the scoreboard were not numbers on the players' uniforms, but corresponded with numbers assigned to the players in the scorecard.

This first Redland Field scoreboard lasted until 1934 when it was extensively remodeled with art deco influences.

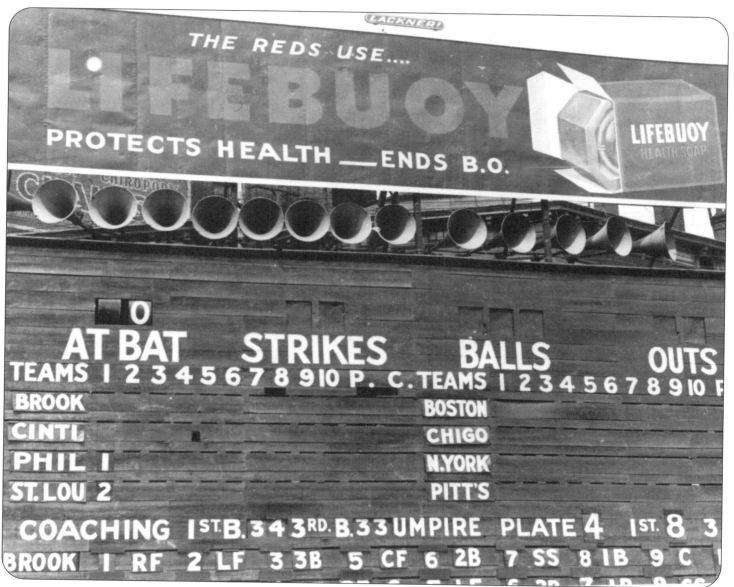

Soldiers, Sopranos, and Scatbacks

Going to a sporting event at Redland/Crosley Field did not always mean a baseball game. Over its 68 years of existence, the ballpark hosted football, boxing, wrestling, rodeo, and even bullfighting.

The ballpark served as an outdoor arena, and attracted many non-sporting events too, including opera, concerts, ice shows, movies, and circuses. Prior to 1900, the city police department staged its annual reviews at what was then called League Park.

One of the more unusual events was the opera "Siegfried," staged at Redland Field in 1916. The reviewer for the *Enquirer* admitted that the roar of the nearby trains and the occasional toot of an automobile horn disturbed the production, but they could not ruin the "genuine pleasure" the performance provided.

During the 1910s and 1920s, movie promoters billed the park as the "Redland Airdome" and showed movies for a nickel. In the 1920s, the park added dances, and the band consisted of a clarinet, sax, piano, and drums. This doesn't sound like the ingredients for trouble, but there were complaints about "vulgar conduct between boys and girls in the unlighted portions of the grandstand," and the events were soon cancelled.

Crosley Field hosted an Ice Capades show in the 1950s, a Wendell Wilkie political rally in 1940, and the Roy Rogers rodeo in the late '40s. The rodeo, which was staged during the baseball season while the Reds were on the road, created numerous problems for groundskeeper Matty Schwab when some unattended horses grazed heavily on the outfield grass.

Many local amateur baseball games were held at Redland/Crosley, and baseball's Negro Leagues played baseball at Findlay and Western in the teens, '20s, '30s and '40s. The original Cincinnati Bengals played there in 1937. ◆

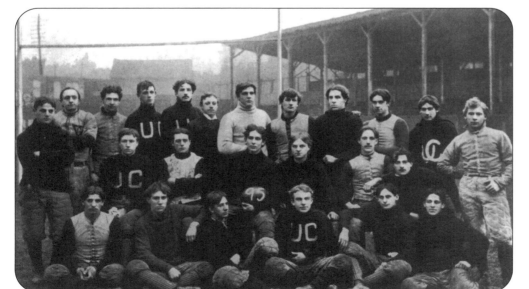

Left: *The University of Cincinnati football team posed in front of the League Park grandstand and a temporary goalpost in the 1890s.*

Right: *During World War I, on October 17, 1917, the Cincinnati Home Guard and police force staged a general review at Redland Field.*

Crosley Field

1919: That Championship Season

For 35 seasons, the old brickyard at Findlay and Western had hosted major league baseball, and despite new grandstands and improved fields, the Reds had never captured a pennant. The combined talents of 20 managers (including such famous baseball names as Buck Ewing, Charles Comiskey, Clark Griffith, and Christy Mathewson) had brought Cincinnati two second place finishes, but more often the club resided in the second division.

Although the team had shown improvement in 1917 and 1918 under Mathewson, the local bugs hardly expected the 1919 Reds to improve on their third place finish of '18. To make matters worse, as the team prepared for the new season, Mathewson, who had shipped out to Europe in the fall of 1918, was missing overseas in France. Club president Garry Herrmann received no response to several cablegrams (Matty was in fact in a hospital recovering from a gas attack that would eventually lead to his death in 1925), and Herrmann finally hired ex-Phillies manager Pat Moran.

To add to the woes, the club had signed several new players over the winter, star outfielder Edd Roush was a contract holdout, and Moran didn't have a shortstop. The team headed to Waxahachie, Texas (30 miles south of Dallas) for spring training with only 13 players. Two weeks of rain robbed the club of much practice time and left them scrambling for dry fields. But the Reds started fast, winning seven in a row and on May 11, Hod Eller threw a no-hitter at Redland, the first in Cincinnati since Noodles Hahn in 1900.

The favored New York Giants took over the lead as the Reds slumped in May and June, setting up a crucial series at Redland in early August. The rabid, pennant-hungry bugs flocked to Redland for the three games. Although small by today's standards, the 13,000 for the Friday game set an all-time attendance record for a Friday game in Cincinnati. Over 22,000 filled the park to capacity on Saturday, and an all-time record crowd of 32,000, 5,000 more than any opener had ever drawn, squeezed into Redland on Sunday. Temporary seats were placed in front of the grandstands and standing-room-only sections were roped off in the outfield. By 2 o'clock President Herrmann deemed the park too full and he ordered the ticket windows closed. A few hundred fans didn't take the news kindly, and with the aid of a ladder, climbed over the left field fence. The Reds won two of the three games, took over first place for good, and clinched the pennant on September 16. ◆

Right: *Pat Moran's entire life was baseball. The Massachusetts Irishman broke into the majors in 1901 as a catcher at the age of 25. He played his last season in 1914; a year later he was manager of the Phillies and he led them to a pennant. He joined the Reds in 1919 under difficult circumstances and immediately led Cincinnati to a 96-44 mark, the best winning percentage ever in club history (.686), and a World Series victory. Five years later, the popular Moran was dead, of Bright's disease, hastened by a chronic drinking problem. His .564 winning percentage with the Reds ranks third behind Sparky Anderson and Buck Ewing.*

Left: *The best third baseman in the National League in 1919 – and one of the best in Reds history – was Heinie Groh. Groh played eight seasons for the Reds from 1914 to 1921 and is best remembered for his "bottle"* *bat. According to baseball historian Lee Allen, Groh used a very wide bat to provide more hitting space, and shaved the handle thin. A fan shouted at Heinie, "What are you using, a bottle?" and the name was born.*

Crosley Field

The Rajah of Redland: Edd Roush

In the deep green pasture that was Redland Field, cantankerous farmboy Edd Roush of Oakland City, Indiana, was the National League's top center fielder of his era (1913-31).

"He and Tris Speaker and Willie Mays are the best I've ever seen at going back on a fly ball," said the late Waite Hoyt, former New York Yankees star pitcher and Reds radio announcer.

There was plenty of ground to go back on at Redland Field – it was a 420-foot smash to straightaway center.

Roush was every bit as intense on the ballfield as another contemporary, Ty Cobb, but only occasionally did he display Cobb's wickedness. Roush was vile only for effect. Once Roush intentionally spiked a Chicago Cub first baseman because the pitcher had knocked down Roush twice at the plate.

Roush's confident bearing rubbed off on his teammates, even when confronting their alleged superiors – such as the 1919 Chicago White Sox in the World Series. Writers said Roush, 26, was the only Red who could have started for the American League winners.

Roush was convinced the Reds would have won without the Black Sox help. "We were better," he said. "I'll believe that to my dying day."

Unlike Cobb, Roush was revered by his teammates. "That Cincinnati club from 1916 to 1926 was one of the nicest bunch of fellows ever gathered together," said Roush.

The fans loved him. In 1969, the 100th anniversary of the club, they voted him the greatest Red of all-time. "I've read where as far as the Cincinnati fans are concerned, I'm the most popular player who ever wore a Reds' uniform," Roush told author Donald Honig in *The Glory of Their Times*. "I don't know about that. It's not for

me to say. But, assuming it's true, I'll tell you one thing: The feeling is mutual."

Roush, 5-foot-11, was a granite-hard 170 pounds even though he disdained formal workouts: he would hold out every spring training, spending the time hunting quail and rabbits at home in Indiana. Roush, a left-handed hitter and thrower, had piercing eyes and a handsome face. There wasn't a worry line on it.

He didn't like playing for the autocratic John McGraw of the New York Giants, but he loved playing for the Reds. "If you made a bad play, (McGraw would) cuss you out, yell at you, call you all sorts of names," said Roush. "That didn't go with me. So I was glad as I could be when he traded me to Cincinnati in the middle of the '16 season. I couldn't have been happier."

It was the same feeling of exhilaration Roush had had seven years earlier, when he escaped his family's dairy barn in Oakland City.

"Winter mornings can be awful cold in Indiana and awful dark," he said. "One of my chores was milking cows, which meant getting up at five o'clock and going out to milk. I don't know whether or not the cows liked it, but I didn't.

"I was playing ball on the town team, so one cold, dark winter morning, I said to myself, 'I'll be a ballplayer.' I didn't really expect to make it all the way to the big leagues, but I didn't care. I just had to get away from them damn cows…."

Just as he could milk cows with both hands, so, too, could Roush throw the ball with either hand. Good thing. When the natural lefthander started playing ball, he had to wear a glove on his left hand – gloves for the right hand were hard to come by in farm towns.

It was a falling out with McGraw which led to Roush's trade to the Reds in 1916 (along with aging pitcher Christy Mathewson and Bill McKechnie). Matty, who immediately took over as manager of the Reds, made Roush his center fielder. Matty loved Roush because of his hard play and integrity.

Fixing games was not unusual in that era – even Ty Cobb and Tris Speaker were chronicled to have done it in one meaningless late season game. For Roush, such behavior was anathema. "Get running you crooked son of a bitch!" he yelled at a Reds teammate who was dawdling on a base in front of him.

Roush's daring, diving catches in the Redland outfield and his extra-base mentality on offense led to a chronically dirty uniform. Baseball in the early 1900s was not the pristine, "clean" game it would later become. When the ball came bounding out to center, Roush, like all outfielders, had to be alert for the unexpected hop.

"The ball wasn't wrapped tight, and lots of times it'd get mashed on one side," said Roush. "I've caught many a ball in the outfield that was mashed flat on one side. Come bouncing out there like a jumping bean. They wouldn't throw it out of the game, though. Only used about three or four balls in a whole game."

Swinging his trademark tree trunk of a bat – it weighed 48 ounces, and was the heaviest bat of the era – Roush led the NL with a .341 average in 1917, his first full season in Cincinnati, and won the batting title again in 1919 with a .321 average. ◆

In 1969, on the 100th anniversary of the beginning of the professional game in Cincinnati, Edd Roush was named the starting center fielder in a fans' poll of the greatest Reds ever. Roush was elected to the Reds Hall of Fame in 1960 and to baseball's Hall of Fame in Cooperstown in 1962. When Roush retired in 1931, he held several club records including most RBI.

Cincinnati's First World Series

The 1919 World Series will forever be remembered as the "Black Sox" series when eight of the Chicago White Sox sold their talents to gamblers and threw the Series. Edd Roush and other Reds never bought the story: "We could have beat them no matter what the circumstances!" Roush later claimed. "The 1919 Cincinnati Reds were better."

Such arguments, though, were unimaginable in late September of 1919, as Cincinnati prepared to host its first World Series. On the eve of the October 1 opening game, Cincinnati's hotels were jammed, and the streets so crowded that the mayor banned automobiles between Sixth and Fourth Streets and Walnut and Vine so that the streetcars could operate safely. Several downtown venues, including Music Hall, Emery Auditorium, and the Sinton Hotel set up temporary seats and charged 50 cents admission to follow the game on hastily erected scoreboards.

Not since the opening of Redland in 1912 had Cincinnati been so crazy for baseball. The financial district was at a standstill. The schools distributed teaching suggestions about the valuable lessons to be learned from the play of the Reds: clean living, quick thinking, good winners and good losers, and strong bodies and healthy minds. Many students, however, chose to take in these lessons first hand at the ballpark and played hooky.

All reserved seats for the first three Cincinnati games were sold in advance. Mindful of the overflow crowds at the yard for the big Giants series back in August, the city closed York Street behind the left field wall and permitted President Herrmann to build temporary bleachers. The sale of unreserved seats began at 10 a.m. on Monday, September 29, and a one-half mile long line stretched around the park.

Eighty-degree temperatures greeted the fans on October 1; by 1:45, all the seats were full and fans stood in the outfield behind ropes watching batting practice. Dutch Reuther, one of the Reds pitchers remembered "Shoeless" Joe Jackson take his cuts: "Up to that time no batter had ever hit a ball on the fly into the right field bleachers; Joe poled three halfway into the bleachers." Youngsters standing in the outfield ducked under the ropes and chased balls that got past the fielders, and the *Enquirer* reported that "many pellets were lost this way."

Patriotic bunting decked the grandstand; John Philip Sousa provided the pre-game music with the national anthem and "Stars and Stripes Forever." The crowd included many baseball club owners, the governors of Ohio, Indiana, and Kentucky, and the singer George M. Cohan. Up in the press box were writers Damon Runyan, Ring Lardner, and a young Westbrook Pegler.

Never was a day more perfect for the club president and consummate host, Garry Herrmann. He set up a fine luncheon spread for his out-of-town guests, featuring burgoo, boiled ham, sauerkraut, and his beloved bratwurst. He had to be pleased by the huge turnout of 30,511, who paid $98,778 to watch the first game.

The Reds, who had a better regular season record than the White Sox, were underdogs, but they dominated the first game, 9-1, and won the second, 4-2. Chicago's starting pitchers in these two games, Eddie Cicotte and Lefty Williams, later admitted they were part of the fix.

The teams traveled to Chicago for games three, four, and five, and the Reds won two of three to take a 4-1 lead in the Series (the Series was a best-of-nine affair in 1919). Games six and seven were played in Cincinnati and the Reds only had to win one to clinch the series. Another huge crowd of over 30,000 filled the park on Tuesday, October 7, but the Reds lost, 5-4, in ten innings. Strangely, only 13,923 showed up the next day, on a day the Reds could have potentially won the Series, but again the

Reds lost. There had been little advance sale of game seven tickets and the walk-up sales on game day were very weak.

The clubs then returned to Chicago where the Reds beat the White Sox the next day, and won the club's first World Series.

Nearly one year later, the gamblers behind the fix and eight Chicago players admitted they played a role in throwing the Series, forever casting a shadow over the Reds victory. But for a few glorious afternoons in October, 1919, when no one imagined such treachery, Cincinnati first tasted the sweetness of a World Series, and Findlay and Western enjoyed its finest moments. ◆

The temporary left field bleachers created a unique backdrop for the Series. This was the only occasion the club ever erected these stands. Reds first baseman Jake Daubert had just singled in game one off Ed Cicotte, one of the eight "Black Sox" later suspended. Two other Chicago players who were also banned for life were left fielder "Shoeless" Joe Jackson and third baseman Buck Weaver.

Below: Greasy Neale, the Reds right fielder was thrown out at second base in the sixth inning of the second game of the 1919 World Series at Redland Field. The White Sox pitcher was Lefty Williams and the shortstop making the tag was Swede Risberg, both active participants in the scandal.

The renegade bleacherites filled every window in the Oliver Schlemmer Company (right) and the Jantz and Leist Electric Company (left), and sat atop the rear wall of the bleachers. This center field scoreboard was erected because the regular left field scoreboard was obscured by the temporary bleachers. Note also the scoreboard style of the time: the Reds are the home team, but are listed above Chicago.

Top Right: This World Series picture was taken by Miriam Dossman, age 16, who attended the first game of the Series with her father. Fans ran about the field, probably celebrating the victory after the game.

Bottom Right: An unknown fan in the right field stands took this photo during the seventh inning of game two. The caption in the photographer's scrapbook reads "Red Going on Field." The player in the foreground was likely right fielder Greasy Neale. This picture was apparently taken just a few moments after Neale was thrown out at second, as shown below.

Crosley Field

The Fourth

1920-1929:
Radio, Rixey, and the Babe

THE REDS BEGAN THE 1920S AT REDLAND AS THE WORLD CHAMPIONS of baseball. More than 30,000 grateful and expectant fans filled the ballpark on April 14, 1920 to see the champs beat the Chicago Cubs 7-3. The enthusiasm for baseball and the hopes for the Reds were at an all-time high on Opening Day, but before the year was out, fans learned the bitter truth about the 1919 Series, and that their championship was tainted. The Reds stumbled on the field, too, never repeating the success of the 1919 season (although they did finish second in 1922, 1923, and 1926), and by the end of the decade were trapped in the second division.

Despite the up and down performance of the club, the Opening Day crowds in the 1920s regularly topped the 30,000 mark and the 1924 opener drew the all-time Redland/Crosley Field record of 35,747. The official capacity of the park, however remained at 20,696 until 1927 when the club added 5,000 new field level box seats. The seats were placed in front of the main grandstand and stretched almost to the outfield fences.

The addition of the new seats required moving home plate out further from the grandstand. This reduced the outfield dimensions some 20 feet. The move was prompted by the renovation, but it happened to coincide with the growing appreciation of the over-the-fence home run, although the distances were still quite long by today's standards.

The original dimensions of 360 to left field, 420 to center, and 400 to right were reduced to 339 to left, 407 to center, and 377 to right.

According to major league rules of the time (1926-1931), however, a batter could be credited with a home run without hitting the ball over the outfield fence. Any fair ball that bounced into the stands beyond 250 feet was a home run. The Reds placed white poles down each line to mark the spot. These "bounced" home runs must have been rare, but in 1927, the Waner brothers, Paul and Lloyd ("Big Poison" and "Little Poison") both managed to

The 1920 Reds raised the 1919 World Championship flag above Redland Field.

A full house of 34,000 fans filled Redland Field on Opening Day, April 16, 1929.

Throughout the 1920s, the club sold advertising on the bleacher wall, but discontinued this practice in the early 1930s.

The white pole appears to be the marker the club placed down each foul line to mark 250 feet from home plate. Any fair ball bouncing into the stands bordering the foul lines beyond the pole was a home run – in front of the pole, a double.

slice line drives into the left field stands on one bounce just beyond the 250-foot marker, *in the same game, and in the same inning!*

In the 1920s, you could see a Reds game for 50 cents out in the right field bleachers, or you could sit in a front row box for $1.50. General admission in the grandstand was $1.10. The club also offered season tickets for eight box seats at $146.30. Through the mid-twenties, these ticket prices included a war tax.

Unlike today, when nearly all box seats are taken by season ticket holders or sold far in advance, good seats were available for almost every game. The Henry Straus Cigar Store, Sixth and Walnut, was the official downtown ticket office.

The average attendance at Redland in the 1920s was 6,226 per game. The club drew 672,987 in 1926, setting a record that would stand until 1938. However, a miserable seventh-place finish in 1929 attracted only 295,000 – an average of only 3,800 per game. Twelve percent of the 1929 attendance was in the stands on Opening Day. ◆

One of the earliest aerial photographs of Redland Field captured an overflow crowd, sometime between 1919 and 1921 (the years the Standard Electric Tool Co. occupied the building behind the left field wall). This was probably an Opening Day game, since fans were on the field, although the club permitted crowds on the field for over-capacity crowds. (It is not the 1919 World Series as there are no temporary bleachers above the left field wall.) Note the fans atop the center field wall, the scoreboard, the roof of the main grandstand, and the roof of the Jantz and Leist Electric Co. across Western Avenue.

Crosley Field

Crosley Field

No "Dipsydoos:" The First Home Runs at Redland

Pat Duncan, a native of Coalton, Ohio, played six seasons as left fielder for the Reds from 1919-1924. He hit the first major league over-the-fence home run at Redland/Crosley Field in 1921.

In 1919, Jack Ryder, the veteran baseball reporter for *The Cincinnati Enquirer*, predicted that no one could hit a pitched ball over the fence at Redland Field. "Several fungo hitters, standing on the home plate at Redland Field, have hit the ball over the center-field wall, an impossible drive for a batter hitting against a pitcher," wrote Ryder.

Ryder was not crazy. He was writing in a "dead ball" era, when spacious ballparks and mushier baseballs made over-the-fence home runs rare. More importantly, Ryder's bias reflected the offensive philosophy of the era, "scientific baseball," in which hitters choked up and aimed their hits, rather than taking big roundhouse wallops.

But within two years, Ryder's prediction, and the world of "scientific baseball" had been shattered by a young hitter from New York named Ruth. The Babe's swing-for-the-fences hitting style began to produce great results in 1919 when he set a home run record with 29, and in the 1920 season Ruth blasted a phenomenal 54 home runs.

Baseball fans no longer dismissed the home run as a fluke, and other players began to swing with more power. Finally in 1921, the ball began sailing out of Redland. But it wasn't a major leaguer who hit the first homer, although he could have been.

On May 22, 1921, John Beckwith, a shortstop playing for the Chicago Giants of the National Colored League, smashed a ball over the left field wall. The homer came against Cincinnati's entry in the league, the Cubans, who rented Redland Field. Beckwith was in the Negro Leagues as a player and manager for 23 years and was one of the leading home run hitters. But his playing career ended before Jackie Robinson integrated baseball in 1947.

One month after Beckwith's blast, on June 21, the Reds left fielder, Pat Duncan, became the first major league player to hit a home run over the fence at Redland Field. Duncan, who played on the 1919 World Series team, connected in the fifth inning against St. Louis. The ball cleared the left center field wall by just five feet and hit a policeman on York Street. Duncan, who possessed good power, but was never a home run hitting star, was however blessed with an innate home run trot. "Pat took his own time about going around the paths, as there was nothing to hurry him," observed Ryder.

Only 1,600 saw Duncan's homer, but one of the faithful left the park, bought a bouquet at a nearby flower shop, and returned to present it to the new home run hero.

Just over a month later, Babe Ruth and the Yankees swept into Cincinnati for an exhibition game. As the cartoon (right) suggests, many fans came to see if Ruth could emulate Duncan's feat. Over 16,000 witnessed the exhibition, and they were not disappointed.

In batting practice, Ruth lifted one over the center field fence. But could he do it in the game? In the fifth, with the bases loaded. Ruth swung at the first pitch and delivered a grand slam over the center field wall. The *Enquirer* estimated the distance as 450 feet. Then, in the seventh inning, Ruth smacked a low line drive over the right center field fence into the bleachers.

Years later, Ruth was still proud of his home runs: "Believe me," he said, "neither of them was a dipsydoo." ◆

Crosley Field

The Reds on Radio

Powel Crosley became a part of Cincinnati baseball when he purchased the Reds in 1934, but even before that, Crosley had made his presence felt at the corner of Findlay and Western.

Crosley, one of the great American entrepreneurs of the 20th century, began his broadcasting ventures in 1921 when he opened his radio manufacturing plant. In 1922, he put WLW on the air, and later acquired WSAI. On April 15, 1924, WLW broadcast the Opening Day game, the first time a Cincinnati station carried a Reds game. The newspapers did not identify the announcers of this historic broadcast, but noted that they "gave all the play-by-play details," and thousands at home "heard" the game on radio. The newspaper reporter put quotes around "heard," apparently unsure of how to describe this novel experience.

Crosley himself moved behind the mike for at least three Opening Day contests in 1926, '27, and '28 when he broadcast play-by-play from the roof of the grandstand. In 1927 and 1928, a second microphone at a table on the field handled player interviews. Crosley arranged to have the players and managers say a "few reassuring words" reported the *Enquirer*. In 1928, Crosley put together an "All-Star" pre-game lineup featuring Commissioner Kennesaw Landis, Reds president C.J. McDiarmid, Cubs owner William Wrigley, Jr., and the Governor of Ohio, A.V. Donahey.

On at least one occasion, Crosley had partners on his broadcasting team, although apparently he did not bring them in for their baseball knowledge. In 1927, he was assisted by a vaudeville team of Ford and Glenn and his orchestra conductor, William Stace.

Although Crosley was a visionary and a marketing genius, these Opening Day games did not cause him to plunge into baseball broadcasting. The Opening Day broadcasts in the 1920s were the *only* games carried all season. Further, Crosley did not try to develop any exclusive arrangement with the Reds. In fact, in 1928, four Cincinnati stations carried the game, including WLW, WSAI, WFBE, and WKRC. It wasn't until 1929 that Crosley had WSAI devote more time to baseball, carrying a few additional games each season, called by Bob Burdette, and it wasn't until the mid-1930s with the arrival of Walter "Red" Barber, that Crosley finally realized the full potential of baseball and radio. ◆

Reds manager Jack Hendricks, who led the club from 1924 to 1929, said a "few reassuring words" to the fans on an early WLW broadcast from Redland Field.

In the '20s, Powel Crosley, Jr. cut a handsome figure about Cincinnati. He was a wealthy businessman who had seen the radio revolution coming and started his own manufacturing company and his own radio station. By the mid-'20s Crosley radios were among the most popular sold in the United States, and WLW was on its way to becoming the "Nation's Station."

But it wasn't always so easy for Crosley. The son of a prominent attorney, young Powel played the part of a dilettante, dabbling in several unsuccessful jobs, most involving the fledgling auto industry. In 1921, Crosley's young son wanted to buy a radio; Crosley, ever the tinkerer, thought he could build one for far less. He did, and soon began making them by the thousands in his factory a few blocks north of Redland Field. With his founding of WLW in 1922, he was on his way to amassing the fortune that would enable him to buy the Reds in 1934.

But in the 1920s, his connection with the Reds was as a fan, as well as the occasional broadcaster of play-by-play on Opening Days from the roof of the grandstand of the baseball park that would eventually bear his name.

The Cuban, Eppa Jeptha, and Bubbles

Eppa Rixey watched in wonder from the Reds bullpen. Eugene "Bubbles" Hargrave did the same from his catcher's position. Reds pitcher Dolf Luque set his glove – the ball still inside it – on top of the mound at Redland Field in Cincinnati.

Nobody, not even Luque, knew for certain what he was going to do.

But Luque knew this: he was going to pay a visit to the dugout of Mr. McGraw's New York Giants, who were burying the young Reds pitcher in a verbal blizzard – much of it, as usual, to do with Luque's Castillian character. He was born and raised in Cuba, one of the few natives light-skinned enough to be playing outside the Negro Leagues.

Luque, 33, his team trailing 6-2 in the eighth inning on a hot August afternoon in 1923, was having a rare off-day. It was coming at a bad time, too. The Reds, who had been in the race with the Giants all season, were about to drop a fifth straight game to them at Redland.

Luque charged the Giants team, which was sitting on a temporary bench in front of the roped-off overflow crowd. Giants outfielder Casey Stengel didn't move. He figured Luque was after Bill Cunningham, who had just gotten off a particularly choice epithet. Luque, however, had his man: the sharp-tongued Stengel. The pitcher delivered a crisp right. It caught Stengel in the head and knocked him off the bench.

The Giants' Ross Youngs, who had been batting and trailed Luque to the Giants bench, pulled the Reds pitcher off Stengel. Two policemen took Luque the rest of the way to the Reds dugout, but it wasn't far enough. After Edd Roush, the Reds center fielder, stirred up the Giants dust with a personal visit of his own, Luque shot back onto the field.

He was carrying a bat.

The police were carrying billy clubs. They retrieved Luque, this time escorting him to the Reds clubhouse. Unfortunately for the Reds, the Cuban's spark produced no fire. The Reds went on to lose the game, and ultimately the pennant by 4 1/2 games with a 91-63 record.

It was no fault of Luque's. Purchased from Louisville, where he went 11-2 in 1918, Luque led the National League with a 27-8 record and a 1.93 ERA in 1923. It was almost a full run better than the 2.80 of Rixey, the league's runnerup. Rixey, who had been acquired two years earlier in a trade with Philadelphia, won 20 games in 1923 after winning 25 in 1922 at age 30. Pete Donohue, like Rixey a college graduate (Texas Christian University) was matinee-idol handsome with a curve ball to match. He won 21 games. The support was good. Roush hit .351, and Hargrave, who was acquired the same year as Rixey when Reds president Garry Herrmann paid $10,000 to the St. Paul, Minnesota, minor-league club, hit .333 and threw out 90 would-be base stealers.

What a wild blend these Reds of the mid-twenties were.

Rixey had walked right off the campus of the University of Virginia, where he majored in chemistry, and into the major leagues. The Phillies were tipped to him by UVA coach Cy Rigler, who was a National League umpire and a Phillies scout. The left-handed Rixey, ever the Virginia gentleman, was born and raised in Culpepper.

"It's funny, you know," "Rixey would later reminisce. "I never had any idea of a Hall of Fame when I started playing with the Culpepper Hurricanes. I was seven years old."

Rixey was the perfect counterpoint to Luque. Rixey was predictable: he won 100 games his first five years with the Reds, 64 the next five. He was steady: he won 266 games overall. He was tall: 6-foot-5. Eppa Jeptha Rixey, he was called. It wasn't even his real middle name.

"Bill Phelon, sports editor of *The Cincinnati Times-Star*, had a flair for poems," explained Rixey. "(After) the third game I won in the NL in 1912…he wrote (a poem) about me. My last name didn't fill out the last line the way he wanted it, so he added to it. He called me 'Eppa Jeptha Rixey.' …People assumed it was right. I've got cousins in Virginia who write me that way. They believe it's my real name. Some of the record books carry it that way."

Luque, on the other hand, wasn't predictable. He lost the most games (23) in the NL the year before he won the most. He wasn't steady: he once threw an ice pick at a teammate, and went after third baseman Babe Pinelli with a pair of scissors when Pinelli had the audacity to suggest to Luque how he might pitch an opposing hitter. Luque's teammates intercepted him, but not before Luque issued Pinelli this ultimatum: "You get taxicab. I get taxicab. Then we get guns and have a duel." And Luque wasn't tall: 5-foot-7.

Eppa Rixey spent 13 seasons with the Reds, and was elected to the Hall of Fame in 1963.

Crosley Field

Unlike Rixey, Luque would never make the Hall of Fame, except the one reserved for hotheads.

Trying to lend some stability behind the plate was Bubbles Hargrave, but this is the same person who, before the 1926 season, had an attack of appendicitis, refused to let the doctors operate, and instead went on a strict diet, eschewing solid food. It trimmed 14 pounds off Bubbles, who said his vision also improved, enough so that he hit .353, and became the first NL catcher in 41 years (since King Kelley) to win the batting title – the first player in seven years to win an NL batting title who wasn't named Rogers Hornsby.

And what was Hargrave's secret?

"Buttermilk," he said.

Whenever he got hungry, he went on a buttermilk binge. Turns out his love affair for buttermilk was long and deep, dating back to his boyhood in New Haven, Indiana, where it was a staple on dining room tables.

The Cuban, Eppa, and Bubbles.

Baseball's equivalent of assault and battery.

Rixey summed it up for all of them years later when he was asked what he thought of night games, something which he and Hargrave and Luque never played.

"I always liked sunshine and sweat for my baseball," said Eppa. ◆

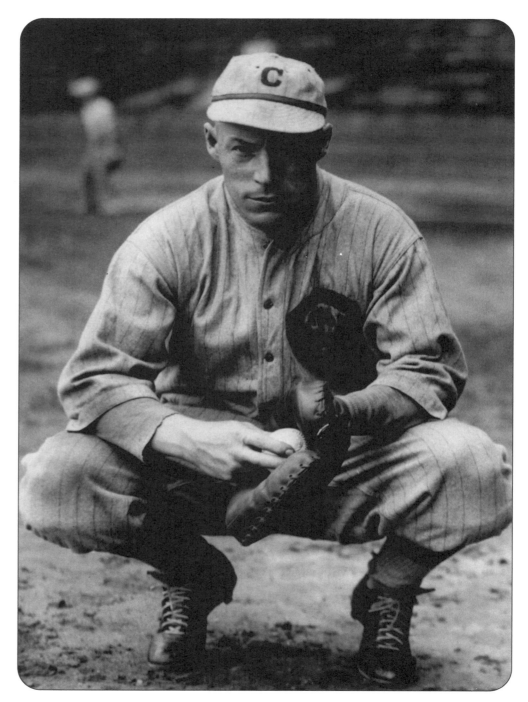

Bubbles Hargrave played eight years for the Reds from 1921-1928 and had six .300 seasons.

Adolfo Luque played 20 seasons, 12 with the Reds. His 27 wins in 1923 set the modern club record (later tied by Bucky Walters).

The Fifth

1930-1939: What a Decade!

N EVER WAS MORE HISTORY MADE AT THE CORNER OF FINDLAY AND Western than in the decade of the 1930s. The team, the ballpark, and the ownership all experienced profound changes, and the most radical innovation of all, night baseball, changed forever the way baseball was played, not just in Cincinnati, but throughout the country.

The decade began with a whimper, the team floundering in seventh place and in the middle of 11 straight second-division finishes, including five trips to the cellar. Sidney Weil, a successful Cincinnati businessman, and a generous owner given the days of the Great Depression (he once offered refunds on Opening Day tickets because the weather was so cold), engineered a couple of excellent trades (picking up Ernie Lombardi and Paul Derringer for practically nothing in return), but he could not put a winning team on the field nor fans in the seats. In 1933, just 218,000 people (an average of 2,868 per game) showed up at Redland, and Weil gave up the fight.

However, no buyer stepped forward, and The Central Trust Co. temporarily took control of the Reds. The bank then had the extreme good sense (or luck) to hire a minor league executive named Larry MacPhail to run the club. The revolution of the 1930s at Redland can be dated from November 7, 1933, the date MacPhail took control.

The aggressive MacPhail knew talent and he immediately recognized the lack of it on the Cincinnati club. He began mapping out a series of trades and acquisitions, but he realized that a conservative bank in the middle of a depression would not be a ready source of cash for his transactions. So MacPhail turned to the local business community and began wooing Powel Crosley, Jr., who had been approached months earlier when Weil announced he was selling the team. At that time, Crosley had turned down the

Ernie Lombardi helped lead the Reds' resurgence in the late 1930s, with his MVP season in 1938. "One of the greatest batters of all time," said Ted Williams.

opportunity, but now with the formidable MacPhail making the pitch, Crosley was persuaded. He was particularly moved by the argument that if someone did not step forward, the club might pass into outside hands and Cincinnati might lose the team.

Crosley was also impressed by the 43-year-old MacPhail. "I was never interested until Mr. MacPhail came into the picture. He has built up an efficient organization and strengthened the club quickly," said Crosley. Wisely, he left the baseball matters to MacPhail, who retained the position of vice president and general manager.

Crosley, 48, was a life-long fan of the Reds, and had played organized baseball with his College Hill neighborhood nine. But the lanky businessman had found more pleasure in tinkering with automobiles, airplanes, and radios and by the 1930s, the success of his radio empire and home appliance business had made him one of Cincinnati's leading industrialists and most prominent citizens.

The baseball deal cost Crosley $175,000 in preferred stock, and in 1936 he purchased an additional 51 percent of the common stock of the club, giving him controlling interest.

Unlike Garry Herrmann, Crosley wanted his name on the ballpark and on April 16, 1934, Redland was rechristened "Crosley Field." Crosley also saw a marketing opportunity, and placed large replicas of a Crosley radio and refrigerator atop the scoreboard. According to broadcaster Red Barber, these signs generated much debate within the club, with a young public relations man, James Reston (later of *The New York Times*), being the most outspoken. Reston soon left the club, perhaps as a result of the dispute, and the signs also came down after just one season. ◆

Sidney Weil (right), owner of the Reds from 1929-1933, conferred with his manager Donnie Bush in 1933. Weil may be the only owner in Reds history to have appeared in a uniform. Weil had the double misfortune of owning a baseball club in the middle of the Depression, and having it be the Reds, who were the worst team in the National League.

Larry MacPhail, manager Charlie Dressen, and Powel Crosley, Jr. posed for this picture in the spring of 1935. Although Crosley had enormous confidence in MacPhail, the first four years of the Crosley-MacPhail partnership (1934–1937) saw the Reds finish eighth, sixth, fifth, and eighth. Dressen, who managed in each of those seasons, was fired during the '37 season, and MacPhail also left to take on the challenge of rebuilding the Brooklyn Dodgers. Crosley chose Warren Giles to replace MacPhail and Bill McKechnie to replace Dressen.

When the Dodgers and Giants moved west in the late 1950s, Crosley received offers from baseball to move the Reds to New York. He never seriously considered the offers. Business manager John Murdough recalled Crosley's position. "Why would I want to go all the way to New York to watch the Reds? I want to watch them at Crosley Field."

Crosley Field

A New Voice in the Catbird Seat

In February of 1934, just two months before Opening Day, Larry MacPhail remained uncertain how many radio broadcasts the club would permit for the 1934 season. Ever the maverick about so many baseball customs, MacPhail could not break away from the fear of most baseball people when it came to broadcasting games: why give away your product? Of course, radio and later television would have just the opposite effect, broadening the sport's appeal, but at the time, baseball men were fearful of radio's impact, especially in the Depression days of the early 1930s when money for tickets was scarce.

MacPhail's new boss, Powel Crosley, a radio man of some renown, had other ideas. Now that Crosley had a baseball team, he wanted it on his radio stations, and in March, WLW hired a 26-year-old announcer from Florida, Walter Lanier "Red" Barber.

Although Crosley believed in radio, he was also wary of over-exposing his baseball team, and Barber only broadcast some 20 games in his first season. Crosley assigned the games to low-powered WSAI, saving his mighty 50,000 (soon to be 500,000) watt WLW for a proven lineup of music, soap operas, and news programs.

Baseball would remain on WSAI during Barber's five seasons in Cincinnati, but the obvious talents and great popularity of Barber soon convinced MacPhail and Crosley to air more games. By 1938, Barber's last year in Cincinnati, WSAI carried most of the Reds' games. Even if a local game was not broadcast, Barber ran a 15 minute preview show live from Crosley Field at 12:15, early enough, MacPhail hoped, to promote the game and entice a few more fans to the park.

With his first broadcast for the Reds on April 17, 1934, Barber accomplished two personal milestones. It was the first major league

game he had ever seen, and it was his first major league broadcast.

He called that game, like all the others he would do at Crosley, from the press box in the first row of the upper deck grandstand behind home plate. He shared the space with reporters and with two other broadcasters, including the popular Harry Hartman, who had been broadcasting a few games each year since 1929 over a rival station, WFBE. Hartman also doubled as the public address announcer.

But it was Barber, who didn't even know how to score a game when he came to Cincinnati, who captured the attention of local fans. In those five Cincinnati seasons, Red took his natural story-teller's art, combined it with a folksy blend of southern expressions and an intense work ethic, and created a style that eventually put him in baseball's Hall of Fame.

Red was at the mike for the first night game in 1935, he broadcast a live remote from the first plane trip ever taken by a major league team in 1934, and he called the first of Johnny Vander Meer's consecutive no-hitters in 1938. No one broadcast the second no-hitter five days later from Brooklyn since the Dodgers banned all radio from 1934-38.

Vander Meer's second no-hitter did teach Red one valuable lesson, however. As news bulletins of Vander Meer's triumph hit Cincinnati airwaves late in the evening, fans gathered in bars to celebrate. After a few steins of lager, many wanted to share the moment with the "Old Redhead," whose number they found conveniently listed in the directory. Barber groggily answered calls until four in the morning, and vowed he would no longer list his name in a phone book.

A poker game provided Red with perhaps the most memorable keepsake of his Cincinnati years. Red unexpectedly lost a hand to friend Frank Koch, a native of southern Ohio. "I had a lock on it," said Koch. "I said I was in the 'catbird seat' all the time, that he didn't have a chance."

Red had never heard the term and Koch explained that it described the catbird, perched high in a tree, confident of capturing its prize. Red, a connoisseur of folk expressions, immediately grasped the spirit of the "catbird seat," and as he later said, "Inasmuch as I had just paid for it, I began to use it." The "catbird seat" became so popular, it is now in the standard dictionaries.

Barber left Cincinnati after the 1938 season and headed for baseball's biggest market, New York. He broadcast for the Dodgers and Yankees before calling his last game in 1965. ◆

Red Barber interviewed an unidentified dignitary during Opening Day ceremonies at Crosley Field in the mid-1930s.

Baseball Under the Lamps

Baseball executives blasted the idea: bush league, not practical, too dangerous, the fans would never accept it. Yet on May 24, 1935, at 8:30 p.m., 632 lamps nestled in eight metal light towers high above Crosley Field, flashed on and night baseball was born.

Baseball under the lights was not a new concept in 1935; demonstrations, including one in Cincinnati in 1909, had been held since the 1880s. The minor leagues had introduced it in 1929. But the major league establishment refused to consider it until Larry MacPhail and Powel Crosley championed the idea.

MacPhail had installed lights in Columbus when he presided over the minor league team there in the early 1930s. He knew night baseball was possible with adequate lighting, and more importantly, night baseball could provide a huge lift at the gate.

The Reds, finishing last in 1933 and 1934, had drawn only 218,000 in 1933 and 207,000 in '34. With attendance problems threatening the existence of the Reds and other clubs, MacPhail lobbied Commissioner Kenesaw Mountain Landis for permission to stage seven games in 1935, one against every other National League club. Landis finally relented, and, at a cost of $50,000, the light towers went up at Crosley.

The first game, against Philadelphia, was scheduled for May 23, and Powel Crosley added to the hype by arranging for his friend President Franklin D. Roosevelt to turn the lights on from a switch at the White House. The new radio network, the Mutual Broadcasting System, also recognized the historic occasion by carrying the game on its national network, broadcast by Red Barber.

Rain postponed the game until Friday, May 24. Perhaps the postponement, the cool temperatures, or a lack of faith in the lights kept the crowd down, for the attendance was below capacity at 20, 422. However, this was a huge crowd by comparison to a regular Friday afternoon game, which would probably have drawn only three to four thousand.

The crowd began arriving at 6:30 for the 8:30 game; many brought picnic suppers, and nearly all carried blankets and overcoats. Four American Legion bands greeted the fans outside the gates, and then the bands moved onto the field where at sunset they gathered by the scoreboard to salute the *lowering* of the flag (which was not flown after dark in the 1930s). MacPhail delighted the crowd with a huge fireworks show that almost backfired. The smoke hung low in the sky in the still air, and along with an intermittent light fog, threatened to obscure the lights.

Finally, at 8:30, a Western Union operator, monitoring the line from the White House, stood at a small table in the first base coaching box. The crowd waited expectantly, the faint glow of the streetlights and house lights of the West End the only faint sparkles in the grays and deep blues of the early evening. When the President touched a telegraph key in Washington, the electric lamps exploded in bright light. Crosley Field basked in the glare, the field suddenly brilliant in green and tan. The fans cheered at the spectacle. Ford Frick, the President of the National League, threw out the first ball, and the Reds, behind the pitching of Paul Derringer, defeated the Phillies, 2-1.

Baseball reporter Frank Grayson of *The Cincinnati Times-Star*, found just one dark area, a shadow along the left field wall. But the overall performance of MacPhail's lighting system answered all questions about the feasibility of night ball. The players and the fans followed the ball easily, and the novelty certainly brought out the best in the reporters. Fly balls shone like "a bald head in a steam room," against the low-hanging clouds, or like a "pearl against dark velvet," against the patches of clear sky. ◆

The light tower in the right field corner was one of eight towers erected in the spring of 1935 for the first night game on May 24. The level of illumination would be substandard today, but the public and the press were satisfied with MacPhail's experiment. Philadelphia center fielder Ethan Allen, a Cincinnati native, was at bat in this photo. The Reds catcher was Gilly Campbell, and Billy Sullivan was at first base. Earl D. Payne, an engineer who designed the lighting scheme, took the photograph.

Crosley Field

Crosley Field

A standing-room-only crowd of 29,105 attended the night game of July 7, 1939, and saw the Reds beat the Cardinals, 7-4. Paul Derringer, who pitched a complete-game win, was at the plate (and about to drive in two runs with a single) when Cincinnati photographer Paul Briol captured the scene.

Baseball under the lights fulfilled every prediction Larry MacPhail had for its success. In the first season of night ball in Cincinnati, the Reds drew 130,337 for seven night games, an average of 18,620. The remaining 69 day games drew 317,910, an average of 4,607. The Reds drew more in their seven night games than some clubs did for the entire season.

Night ball clearly offered a weekday opportunity for working fans to attend a game. As one reporter put it, "A fellow up around Batavia or Pisgah can finish his spring plowing, unhitch ole Dobbin, have supper, and get into town in time to see the night game, lift a few sidles (sic) of beer, and be in the hay again by midnight."

The greatest slugger of all thought he wouldn't enjoy a regular schedule of baseball under the lamps. Two days after the first night game, Babe Ruth, playing for the Boston Bees of the National League, came to Cincinnati, and the slugger was asked about night baseball by Frank Grayson of the Times-Star.

"I'm not in favor of it," he grunted. "Hard on the eyes and a darned sight harder on the digestion. Fellow is under a strain all the time and when a game is finished it is couple of hours before he can inhale a porter-house steak. If he tried it too soon, he is going to be tied in a knot."

Ruth need not have worried about playing much night ball, for that Sunday, May 28, 1935, at Crosley Field, Ruth went back on a line drive to left field. As he started up the steep terrace, his legs buckled and he ducked as the ball landed just behind him. He took himself out of the game, and retired after just one more game.

Despite the success of night ball in Cincinnati, the major leagues were slow to adopt the innovation. The second club to install lights was the Dodgers in 1938, and that came only after Brooklyn hired a new general manager: Larry MacPhail. Most clubs added lights in the 1940s; the Chicago Cubs at Wrigley Field were the last to do so in 1988.

A Wild Night at Crosley

The Reds scheduled the sixth night game of 1935 on July 31 against St. Louis. Larry McPhail anticipated another big evening crowd of 20,000. But the continuing novelty of night baseball combined with the attraction of the World Champion Cardinals produced the wildest game ever at Findlay and Western, not for the performance of the players, but for the tumult of the crowd.

The official attendance was reported as 30,001, but veteran baseball reporters estimated the crowd at over 35,000. Unlike an Opening Day when the club anticipated a sellout, McPhail had too few ushers and police on hand to control the crowd. Many who bought standing room tickets grabbed unoccupied grandstand seats and refused to leave. When 2,500 fans from Dayton on a special excursion train arrived late, many found their seats occupied. Fights erupted over seats, and finally the club allowed the overflow to sit on the field in foul territory. As the game progressed, the crowd on the field moved steadily down the foul lines toward home plate where they stood nine or ten deep, blocking the dugouts and the view of the managers.

Manager Chuck Dressen of the Reds could only follow the game by looking at the scoreboard. "I see the Cardinals got a run," he said at one point, "but I don't know how they got it."

In the fourth inning, irate fans, upset over losing their seats, occupied short right field. The game was delayed 15 minutes until a phalanx of police and ushers chased them off.

In the eighth inning, while time was called to attend to two Cardinal outfielders who collided chasing a ball, a young woman named Kitty Burke jumped out of the crowd near home plate, grabbed a bat and stood in the batter's box, daring St. Louis pitcher Paul Dean to throw her a ball. Dean lobbed her a soft one, and she grounded weakly to first. Burke, a Cincinnati night club entertainer, later went on the burlesque circuit as the only woman

to ever have "batted" in a Major League game.

The game was witnessed by Commissioner Landis, who was the guest of Powel Crosley. Amazingly, neither Landis nor Crosley made any effort to halt the game despite the risk of injury to the fans on the field. Perhaps the most serious threat to the spectators came from Reds pitcher Paul Derringer, who roamed the dugout area with a bat in hand to keep boisterous fans at bay.

And the game? The Reds won 4-3 in the 10th inning. ◆

The Cincinnati Post *ran this photograph of the wild crowd at Crosley Field on its front page on August 1, 1935. The fans on the field* completely blocked the view from the dugouts and from the field boxes.

A Little Water on the Field

Skimming for catfish from the box seats at Crosley Field? It was possible during the flood of 1937.

Cincinnati's worst natural disaster, the flood of 1937, began the third week of January, with the Ohio River rising rapidly. The Millcreek, a small tributary of the Ohio, flowing south along the western edge of downtown, quickly spilled over its banks as high water from the Ohio backed up the creek.

The waters of the Millcreek crept eastward and within a few days had invaded the homes and business of the West End, including Crosley Field, less than one-half mile from the Millcreek.

Years before, groundskeeper Matty Schwab had installed a grid of drains beneath the outfield to drain moisture off the field. But when the Ohio River reached 55 feet, the storm sewers began to back up, and water moved up the drains and onto the field. At 57 feet the water covered the lower levels of the field, and at 60 feet, home plate was inundated.

Soon, the water reached the seats, and by January 26, with the Ohio River at an all-time record level of 80 feet, Crosley Field was under 21 feet of water.

The outfield fence was submerged, and in one of the most memorable moments in Crosley Field history, pitchers Gene Schott and Lee Grissom, along with Schwab, rowed a boat down Western Avenue and right over the center field fence.

Faced with an enormous cleaning job, Schwab resorted to his famed German ingenuity. As the flood receded, Schwab and his crew began hosing down the seats and grandstand walls, washing off the mud and sheen left by the flood. By the time the water was out of the grandstand, the seats were nearly in a game-ready condition. Once the water receded below 55 feet, Schwab's drains accelerated the draining of the field. The only serious damage to the facility was in the newly constructed commissary under the stands where cooking equipment and provisions were ruined. ◆

Early in January of 1937, flood waters invaded Crosley Field, backing up onto the field through the drains under the field. The streets around the park were still dry, but within a few days after this photo was taken, the flood waters covered the center field wall, and all the surrounding streets.

Crosley Field

Reds pitchers Lee Grissom and Gene Schott and groundskeeper Matty Schwab pulled the all-time Crosley Field practical joke when they floated a skiff up Western Avenue and over the center field wall at the height of the 1937 flood. Schott was missing from the above photo, but Grissom tipped his hat to the photographer while Schwab smiled, perhaps relieved that for once events were even beyond his control.

Grissom may well have been the instigator of the stunt. Reds historian Lee Allen wrote that the big southpaw combined "the best features of Rube Waddell and various Ring Lardner characters."

On Opening Day, 1937, just 90 days after the flood waters covered the field, Crosley was in excellent shape. The only reminders of the flood were markers painted on grandstand beams, the scoreboard, and the center field flagpole. (After the 1913 flood, the club painted a line on the left field wall marking the high water mark, but the Chamber of Commerce asked Garry Herrmann to remove it.)

As damaging as the 1937 flood was, no games were cancelled. But in 1940, Crosley Field became the first and only ballpark to have a game called on account of flooding. Although the crest of April 23, 1940, only reached 58 feet, the outfield was covered by a foot of water and two games between the Reds and the Cardinals were postponed.

Southeast of Crosley Field, downtown Cincinnati was barely visible in rain and clouds of January 1937. The floodwaters that filled Crosley came from the Millcreek, visible along the lower edge of the photograph.

At the height of the flood, home plate was under 21 feet of water. In this photo, the flood waters had breached the outfield wall along Western Avenue and inundated the surrounding neighborhood.

A New "NL" Team at Crosley: The Negro Leagues

They came in through the back door at Crosley Field after the Cincinnati Reds had already gone out the front.

"They" were the Cincinnati Tigers, the Queen City's entry in the now famous Negro Leagues of 1936-37.

The Reds knew there was a Negro League team in town, but they didn't know the Tigers played doubleheaders at Crosley Field on weekends when the primary tenants were away. "I never had occasion to cross paths with (the Tigers)," said Eddie Joost, a shortstop and utility infielder with the Reds from 1936 to 1942. "I just had no idea."

The Reds also didn't know the Tigers wore their old uniforms or that the Tigers would have beaten them at their own game.

Outfielder Neil Robinson, a Negro League great, began his career here. He was the best young slugger in town. "Robinson belongs in Cooperstown," said Phil Dixon, author of the acclaimed book, *The Negro Baseball Leagues.* "He had all the tools. Run, throw, field, and hit for power."

Among the Tigers pitchers were Jesse Houston, Porter Moss, and Roy Partlow. They were all born in Cincinnati. They were as good a threesome as any city in America produced in the 1930s – and the best trio, by far, that Cincinnati has produced simultaneously.

"Moss was so tough because he threw submarine style and was just murder on those right-handed hitters," said Tigers manager and catcher/relief pitcher Ted "Double Duty" Radcliffe. "Partlow was the best athlete – he could've made it as a hitter – but for my money Houston was the guy I wanted on the mound. He won 23 games for me in '37."

The Tigers were founded in the fall of 1934 by Cincinnati track star DeHart Hubbard, the first black American to win an Olympic gold medal (broad jump, 1922). There was a passel of local talent to choose from, most of it from the Excelsiors, Hubbard's fine black amateur team. Among them, the Harris brothers, Virgil and Sonny, the pitchers, Houston and Moss. Josh Johnson came down from Pittsburgh, Marlin Carter up from Texas, and Neil Robinson down from Grand Rapids, Michigan.

"In 1935, we rode to games in cars, but in '36 we bought an old Studebaker bus (see photograph, page 89) that belonged to the musical group, the McKinney Cotton Pickers," said Johnson, the Tigers catcher.

"The brakes weren't much. You had to shift down to stop it. I know…I drove it. One year I held out for an extra $10 a month, to go with the $90 a month they had already offered me. The only way I could get the extra $10 was to be assistant bus driver."

The Tigers routinely drew between 5,000 and 10,000 fans to Crosley Field, sometimes as many as 15,000 for the big-name teams. The top musicians of the era – among them Louis Armstrong and Billy "Bojangles" Robinson – came out to Crosley Field.

"One day, Lionel Hampton came out to shag balls in the infield," recalled Tigers third baseman Marlin Carter. "He loved baseball. I lent him my glove. He booted a ball and threw my glove in the dirt. I said, 'Mr. Hampton, do I come in your house and throw your vibes out the window if I mess up a note? Don't be doin' that to my glove!'"

Edgar Bradley, who was a cabdriver, saw the Tigers play at Crosley Field in the 1930s and the Cincinnati Clowns, another Negro League team, play there in the 1940s. At Negro League

The 1936 Cincinnati Tigers posed in front of their bus behind the visitors' clubhouse on the west side of Crosley Field. The left field stands are in the background. The Tigers wore hand-me-down uniforms from the Reds and these appear to be the Reds road uniforms from 1935.

games, he said, you didn't keep the foul balls. Tickets cost less, so you were expected to throw back the foul balls. Generally, there was more of a picnic atmosphere at Tigers and Clowns games than at Reds games. It was more of a social event – a happy get-together on Saturday and Sunday afternoons – because the games came about so rarely. People dressed up.

Josh Gibson was probably the all-time gum-chewing stopper in the history of the Negro Leagues, according to Bradley. "When he came up to bat, everything stopped," said Bradley. "I saw Josh hit the longest ball ever hit over the laundry building in left field. Not even those boppers the Reds had here in the '50s and '60s ever topped it. If Josh had been a Red, he'd have had more suits than Arsenio Hall."

In 1936-37, Gibson and Satchel Paige of the Pittsburgh

Crawfords formed the greatest battery in the history of the Negro Leagues. Tigers fans got to see some of that. There was inter-league play. "I was more partial to the Homestead Grays, though," said Bradley. "They were the sharpest team I ever saw. The ladies really liked 'em, too. Even their road uniforms were always fresh-pressed. They were class."

Moses Hudson, who migrated to Cincinnati from Mississippi in 1932, was a regular visitor to Crosley Field for Negro League games in the 1930s and '40s and integrated baseball in the '50s and '60s.

"My favorite experience of 'em all – and I've seen baseball on all levels – was the Clowns at Crosley," he said. "I swear I could smell the grass growin' during a light rain….The style of play was nice and loose, the way I learned to play it." ◆

Vandy Makes History

Late on the afternoon of Saturday, June 11, 1938, 23-year-old Johnny Vander Meer eyed the Boston Braves hitter, standing in the reddish clay of the batter's box at Crosley Field.

One out away from a no-hitter.

None of the 5,814 fans knew how lucky Vander Meer was even to be here. He should have been dead. In the summer of 1930, his appendix had ruptured. By the time doctors had operated on it, 30 days later, 15-year-old Johnny had peritonitis – an inflammation of the membrane which lines the abdominal cavity. There were no drugs to treat it. Cowboy actor Tom Mix got peritonitis the same day as Vander Meer, and Mix was dead within three days.

Vander Meer fell so far behind in school, he went to work instead. Gradually, he blossomed from a frail boy of 110 pounds, to a strong, wiry, 175-pounder of 17. He and his left arm were famous around Patterson, New Jersey. "Johnny the Cannon" he was called. He threw five no-hitters that year. His parents, immigrants from the Netherlands, didn't like him playing so much ball, but when they saw his love for the game, they let him go.

Vandy played four years in the minors and in 1936, he was named "Minor League Player of the Year." When he walked into the Reds clubhouse at Findlay and Western Avenues in the spring of 1937, he wasn't scared.

"But the the biggest thrill of my life was when I got my own locker and my own uniform with my name on it. It was the very thing I was dreaming about."

Control problems sent Vandy down to Syracuse for most of the '37 season. The next spring he was back with the Reds in Tampa and manager Bill McKechnie was ready for him. McKechnie brought in former pitching great Lefty Grove, who himself had overcome severe control problems, to tutor his young left-hander.

"Johnny," began Lefty, "I was wild because I let the ball go too soon and was not following through. I decided to follow through with my pitch regardless of where the ball went. Every pitch, I followed through so much that I made my left forearm strike my right knee." Vander Meer's control began to come around. By June, his spot in the Reds'

Lew Riggs, Cincinnati third baseman, scooped up a slow bounder from Boston pinch hitter Heinie Mueller and threw on to first base for the final out of Johnny Vander Meer's first no-hitter. Vander Meer watched from the left of the mound.

rotation was secure, and so, too, was his spot in history.

Vandy dipped low, rocked high. Another ground ball! Vandy had done it! His first no-hitter in the major leagues, and the first for the Reds since Hod Eller's in 1919.

Four days later, Vander Meer, pitching in front of his parents and 500 well-wishers from his hometown, took the mound in Ebbets Field for the first-ever night baseball game in Brooklyn.

At first the Brooklyn fans razzed him, but by the eighth inning, they were cheering. After walking the bases full in the ninth, McKechnie came to see him.

"Relax…Take your time…Remember your follow through," he told him. Vandy got the 26th out on a force-out at home and then popped out Leo Durocher to shallow center. Two no-hitters in a row!

In 1971, Vander Meer's consecutive no-hitters were voted by sportswriters as the greatest sporting feat of the 20th century. Nothing has happened since to change it.

"Somebody might tie the record some day," said Vandy, smiling. "But three consecutive no-hitters? I don't think so." ◆

1938: The Stars Come Out to Play

The anxious, star-struck fans began arriving at Crosley Field 18 hours before game time, a quartet of lads from Dayton heading the line. Others came from Indiana, Louisiana, Iowa, and even Idaho. They came to see their heroes, Feller, Ott, Foxx, and the new pitching sensation, Johnny Vander Meer.

They came to see the sixth annual All-Star Game, held in Cincinnati on July 6, 1938.

By game time on Wednesday afternoon, 27,067 filled the yard, a good crowd of 1,000 over capacity, but far short of a typical Opening Day. Ticket prices were not to blame, as the club charged its regular prices ranging from $2 for box seats to 60 cents for the bleachers. The scalpers up and down Western Avenue commanded higher prices: up to $15 for reserved seats and $3 for the bleachers.

Matty Schwab had the ballpark dressed up with patriotic bunting and a temporary expansion of the press box on the roof of the grandstand. The crowd came well-dressed, too. Nixson Denton of the *Times-Star* reported that even the bleacherites, who usually scorned the "namby-pamby earmarks of civilization, such as collars and ties…," had dressed up like gentlemen.

The vendors worked the crowd, selling a bizarre assortment of orangeade, pillows, ice cream, miniature baseballs, sun-shade hats, hot dogs, player dolls, sun glasses, programs, and large, inflated snakes.

The early arrivals took in quite a show at batting practice. "Mr. Dimaggio, Mr. Gehringer and the rest of the boys lost enough balls on Western Avenue to supply most of the sporting goods

Chicago Cubs outfielder Stan Hack scored the first run of the 1938 All-Star Game in the first inning on a sacrifice fly by the Cardinals' Joe Medwick. Mel Ott of the Giants (left) welcomed Hack. Bill Dickey of the Yankees was the catcher and Hall of Famer Bill Klem the umpire.

stores in this section of the Republic," wrote Denton. Jimmy Foxx hit a couple of shots over the roof of the laundry beyond left field.

In the mid-1930s, the American League dominated baseball, having won the 1935, 1936, and 1937 World Series and four of the first five All-Star Games. Even though Babe Ruth had retired, the American League still had the big stars: Jimmy Foxx, Lou Gehrig, Joe Dimaggio, Charlie Gehringer, Bill Dickey, Lefty Grove, Lefty Gomez, and Bob Feller. Cincinnati fans would see eight future American League Hall of Famers on the field this day.

The National League had its share of stars as well; future Hall of Famers Mel Ott, Joe Medwick, and Billy Herman started. But the faithful Reds fans were more interested in their own All-Star starters: right fielder Ival Goodman, catcher Ernie Lombardi (another Hall of Famer), first baseman Frank McCormick, and the

Traditional bunting graced the grandstand for the 1938 All-Star Game. Red Barber broadcast the game from the expanded rooftop press box.

newest star in baseball, Johnny Vander Meer. Just three weeks had elapsed since Vandy pitched his second no-hitter; he was quickly named to the squad and chosen as the starting pitcher.

If Vandy was nervous, the 23-year-old didn't show it. He pitched three shutout innings, and received the biggest hand of the afternoon after getting the last out in the third.

The National League, buoyed by Vandy's great start, took the early lead and won, 4-1. Each of the Reds contributed to the victory: Lombardi had two hits and an RBI; McCormick one hit and an RBI; Goodman made a great catch in the ninth; and Vandy picked up the win.

Lombardi caught the entire game, and said he lost 14 pounds. But he wasn't concerned. He told the writers that he'd make it up with a big steak and a couple of beers after the game.   ◆

Crosley's New Look for the Thirties

The appearance of Crosley Field that fans remember from the 1950s and 1960s was essentially created in the 1930s with several significant changes at Findlay and Western.

Lights: Eight light towers were erected in 1935, one at the end of each foul line, one behind the scoreboard, one behind the sun deck, and four on the grandstand roof.

Expanded Terrace: The outfield terrace, one of Crosley's most defining characteristics (and most exasperating feature for many visiting outfielders) was extended from left field to center and right. The steep left field section had existed since the park was built in 1912. The more gradual center field and right field sections were added by the club after the infamous night game of July 31, 1935, at the suggestion of groundskeeper Matty Schwab. Schwab proposed extending the terrace to provide up to 6,000 temporary seats to accommodate standing-room-only crowds. The job was completed by early September, 1935.

Press Box: Prior to 1937, the press occupied the first rows of the upper deck grandstand behind home plate. The new press box on top of the grandstand roof opened for the 1937 season, and the *Enquirer*

reported that the "scribes" approved of their new quarters. "The place is pretty ritzy, and it should be for $7,800. It has room for 65 people and has everything except a shower bath and a beer spigot."

The press box was expanded temporarily for the 1938 All-Star Game and the 1939 and 1940 World Series, so that it stretched nearly from one end of the grandstand roof to the other, and accommodated over 200 people.

Double Decked Stands (below): In 1939, the Reds challenged for the pennant for the first time in over a decade, and the club had several sell outs. In September of 1939, when it appeared the club

In 1938, the club moved home plate 20 feet closer to the fences and shifted the diamond toward right, moving the left field line 27.6 feet. After 1938, the club reported its center field dimension as 383 feet, but the actual distance to dead center was 375 feet, the shortest in baseball.

would play in the World Series, Powel Crosley added an upper deck to each pavilion, increasing the park's capacity by 3,000 seats to 29,401.

Shorter Fences: In 1938, the Reds reduced the dimensions of the park by moving home plate 20 feet closer to the fences. The great offensive explosion of the 1930s had bypassed Crosley Field, which boasted some of the longest fences in the major leagues. The new distances (shown in the photo above) had the desired effect. The Reds home run total increased to 110 home runs in 1938, the highest total in their history.

The only change to the outfield distances after 1938 came with the addition of the "Goat Run" in the 1940s and 1950s which reduced the right field line another 24 feet.

Foul Pole Screens: In the fall of 1939, Crosley Field became the first major league park to mount screens on the foul poles, the result of a controversial home run hit by Reds center fielder Harry Craft in New York. The *Enquirer* correctly predicted that the screens "will probably be universal in the majors shortly." ◆

Frank McCormick and the 1939-40 Reds

The Reds halcyon days of the late teens to the mid-1920s had been produced through the fiery play of farm boy Edd Roush and the front-office direction of gustatory August "Garry" Herrmann. But the fading glory had faded fully by 1927. Herrmann traded the increasingly cantankerous Roush, and then himself resigned.

So ended the era of Eddie and the Sausage King.

With Roush's departure went the soul of the Reds. From 1927-37, they finished in the second division 11 times, five times in the cellar. The Reds' only solid players were catcher Ernie Lombardi (since 1932) and pitcher Paul Derringer (since 1933). Shortstop Billy Myers and right fielder Ival Goodman arrived in 1935; second baseman Lonny Frey after the 1937 season. First baseman Frank McCormick and center fielder Harry Craft, who had starred the previous season for Syracuse, the Reds' top farm club, were in the Reds camp in 1938. New manager Bill McKechnie and second-year general manager Warren Giles traded for pitcher Bucky Walters in June 1938, and bought the contract of holdout third baseman Billy Werber in spring training, 1939. Rookie pitcher Junior "Gene" Thompson was already in camp. In 1940 came the final pieces: pitchers Joe Beggs, Jim Turner and the mid-season addition of Jimmy Ripple, a freckle-faced, slash-hitting left fielder.

"We were a good-hitting club, but our strength was in the defense – by that I mean pitching and defense," said Thompson, who went 13-3 in 1939 for the pennant-winning Reds. "Ernie Lombardi was a great hitter; he would have easily hit .400 if he wasn't so doggone slow. But Frank McCormick was the ultimate RBI guy. Ernie overshadowed Frank because 'Lom' was so loveable — a lumbering, massive guy who the fans just took to. Frank never got the credit that he deserved. He was never one to attract attention. He was probably the most unheralded player on

that ballclub. He just did the job, day after day after day. But he was the best money player I ever saw. If he had done it for a while longer, he would have been a Hall of Famer."

Maybe McCormick would have been a Hall of Famer had the Reds not waited so inordinately long to bring him up from the minors. (His first four seasons in the minors he hit .347, .280, .381 with 138 RBI, and .322.) He led the National League in hits his first three seasons, and drove in 106, 128, and 127 runs. In defense of the Reds, they thought the rookie was 23; in reality, he was 25. A 1944 Reds newsletter lists the birthdate McCormick gave them as June 9, 1913. The *Baseball Encyclopedia*, which uses official birth records, lists McCormick's DOB as June 9, 1911. McCormick won the Most Valuable Player award in 1940 (following fellow Reds Lombardi, 1938, and Walters, 1939). The Reds thought their newest MVP was 27; he was really 29. He wouldn't have another big year until 1944, when he hit .305 with 102 RBI, at age 33.

There were other things not many fans knew. McCormick, despite his Irish surname, was Polish-American. "We kidded him about that all the time," said Thompson, laughing. Werber, in his 1978 book, *Circling the Bases*, wrote that McCormick, who was born and raised in New York City, took the Irish surname of his mother's second husband.

"Buck" McCormick was strong, tall (6-foot-4), and matinee-idol handsome, with black hair, brown eyes and a square jaw. In the book, *Baseball When The Grass Was Real*, he told about trying to break into pro ball in 1932.

"I worked out with the Giants for a whole week (at the Polo Grounds)," he wrote. "Bill Terry had just taken over. I'd been working in the shipping room of an art gallery in New York. One day I was holding some Early American glass, a cream pitcher and a sugar bowl. They were worth about $450. Well, somebody attracted my attention, and I sort of bumped them together and broke them. Some pair of hands! I got fired. It was soon after that I went up to the Polo Grounds (to try out for Terry)....I thought I did all right, but they said to me, 'Son, if you have a good job, keep it.'"

But McCormick couldn't give up baseball. In 1934, he hopped a bus to a Reds' tryout camp in Beckley, West Virginia. His Bronx-team coach, George Halpern, suggested to the young outfielder that he buy a first baseman's mitt because "there's going to be about 150 kids down there at camp, and a lot of them are going to be outfielders." McCormick took the advice.

"Frank was an unorthodox first baseman," said Thompson. "He wasn't fancy, but there wasn't a better first baseman anywhere. He'd improvise wonderful things like backtracking over first base into foul territory to catch a short-hop throw on a full hop. He was able to judge the speed of the baserunner. He was unorthodox at bat, too. He hit 'down' on the ball. He wasn't a

hard-swinger. He was a pure line-drive hitter, and there was nobody you wanted up there in the clutch more than Frank. What a cleanup hitter."

Wrote Werber: "His (only) shortcoming lay in his almost-exclusive interest in hitting. On numerous occasions, with more effort, he could have converted singles into doubles and, with body blocks, broken up double plays."

Eddie Joost, a utility infielder, said that McCormick's somewhat "reserved" personality kept him from getting the recognition he deserved. Thompson agreed, noting that McCormick, while being a well-spoken gentleman and well-liked, was not "colorful."

"Frank was a great family man, the best in the world," said Thompson. "He wasn't a high roller. He wasn't a down home-country boy who'd go hunting with us during the off-season. He didn't feel like the world owed him a living. Frank was Frank. It's the best way I can explain it." ◆

Frank McCormick addressed the crowd at Crosley Field in 1941, thanking them for the gift of a new car on the occasion of his 1940 MVP award. Mayor James Garfield Stewart was on McCormick's left. McCormick became a Reds broadcaster in the 1960s.

"Schnozz"

The most popular player in the history of Crosley Field was Ernesto Natali Lombardi, born on April 6, 1908 in Oakland, California, the son of Italian immigrants. Ernie quickly became known for his huge hands and skill at ball sports. One of the first games he mastered was bocci – his father's game, the game of the Italians, a lawn bowling game played with balls the size of grapefruits. "Bocci," his friends called him.

He tore up the Pacific Coast League, where a persistent blister on the pinky of his throwing hand caused him to adopt his trademark interlocking grip. In 1931, the 23-year-old Lombardi broke the major-league surface with the Brooklyn Dodgers, and the Reds acquired him the following season. In his 10 seasons (1932-41) in Cincinnati, he averaged .311. From 1935 through 1938, he hit .343, .333, .334, and .342, the last of those winning the batting title, despite hitting into a league-record 30 double plays. He was named the NL's Most Valuable Player that year.

Massive in size, the 6-foot-3, 240-pound Lombardi was revered by his teammates. It was his easy-going disposition, his equanimity. Teammates who couldn't stand one another shared a bond with Lom. "Everybody loved him," said Reds pitcher Bucky Walters.

Lom made everybody feel at home, even the rookies. "Hey kid, got enough money?" he'd ask them before the season's first road trip. Then, without waiting for an answer, he'd push a twenty on them. He just wanted them to be able to feel like big-leaguers.

Lom was a man's man, but nobody swooned over him like the ladies. They flocked to Ladies' Days and shrieked with joy at every lumbering move he made. They waited outside the clubhouse to catch his eye, throw him a smile, ask for a date. Lom, shy as could be, hid inside, talking to the trainers, Doc Rohde and Larry McManus.

"With that pair of good fellows, Ernie felt at home," wrote Lee Allen. "The sight of him, nearly nude, draining a bottle of beer with gargantuan gusto, would have moved a painter or sculptor to a masterpiece of massive realism."

Ted Williams said Lombardi hit the hardest line drives of any right-handed hitter he ever saw and would have hit .400 if he wasn't so slow. Most catchers run like they are carrying a piano on their back. Lombardi ran like he was carrying the piano – and the guy who tuned it.

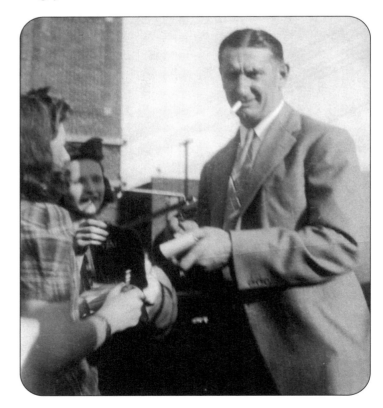

A popular spot for autograph seekers after a game was in the parking lot west of Crosley Field, and "Schnozz" was a favorite target.

Infielders played him 20 feet into the outfield. "It took me four years to find out Pee Wee Reese was a shortstop," said Lombardi. Outfielders threw him out at first base. An umpire once called him out at third on a tag-up from second. When Lom protested, the umpire said: "C'mon, Lom! I know there's no way you could have beaten the throw legitimately. You must have left early!" The day Lombardi beat out a hit to Leo Durocher, the Dodgers' shortstop immediately retired. "Cut the uniform off me," sighed The Lip.

Lom was slow behind the plate, too, leading the league in passed balls for 10 of his 17 seasons. But he was able to compensate for his lack of quickness with strong snap throws which allowed him to pick baserunners off first and third without leaving his crouch.

Lom had a wonderful smile. He could laugh at himself. Teammate Bill Werber wrote that Schnozz snored so loudly, the Reds players made him sleep in the Pullman car reserved for the press. Lom wasn't sensitive about his enormous nose. He let Stengel pose next to it with a ruler. What Lombardi was sensitive about was being perceived as some sort of illiterate Palooka, just because he was big and quiet. He wouldn't sign autographs – until one day he turned down some boys and one turned to another and said, "See, I told you he couldn't write." Lombardi grabbed the pen and signed. Others would trick him again. It bothered him.

Just as it bothered him when the baseball writers did not elect him to the Baseball Hall of Fame. It took the Veterans' Committee to do it. Respect, that is all Lom wanted. Not adoration. He died in the Bay Area in 1978. Eight years later, they hung his plaque in Cooperstown.

Ernest Natali Lombardi…it began.   ◆

Lombardi relaxed in a New York hotel on the eve of the 1939 World Series.

The 1939 Series: You "Snooze," You Lose

The 1939 World Series opened in New York, and the Reds quickly fell behind two games to none. But despite the poor start, Cincinnati was not going to let that interfere with the thrill of hosting a World Series for the first time in 20 years. All reserved seats for games three and four were sold, and by the early evening

Two Hall of Fame managers, Joe McCarthy (left) and Bill McKechnie shake hands prior to game three of the 1939 series at Crosley.

of October 6, some 18 hours before game time, 500 people camped along Western Avenue to buy bleacher tickets.

Peanut and hot dog vendors worked the crowd, and dozens of automobiles slowly cruised the streets taking in the pre-game atmosphere. The intersection of Western Avenue and Findlay Street resembled the busy "shopping district of a small country town on a Saturday night," reported the *Enquirer*. Downtown, the hotel lobbies and sidewalks filled with local and out-of-town fans. Even the national headquarters of the "Hoboes of America" held an open house at its headquarters on West Liberty.

Although over 34,000 had filled Crosley just ten days before for the pennant-clincher, the crowd for game three reached only 32,723, which was still standing-room-only. Cabs let loose a steady stream of passengers near the park. After 11 a.m. it was impossible to hail a cab (even at 50 cents a ride, double the usual fare) and many fans thumbed rides in private cars.

Prior to the game, the hundreds of photographers and reporters on the field focused on the Yankees. Although not as famous as the 1927 squad, the '39 Yankees are rated one of baseball's best teams, and featured six Hall of Famers: catcher Bill Dickey, center fielder Joe Dimaggio, pitchers Red Ruffing and Lefty Gomez, and manager Joe McCarthy. But the most famous Hall of Famer of the '39 Yankees did not play in the 1939 series. Lou Gehrig, inactive since the discovery of his disabling disease earlier in the season, accompanied the team as a non-playing captain, but still drew the most attention from the autograph seekers.

Going into game three, the Yankees had won seven straight World Series games, and had won the Series the past three seasons. Rookie Gene Thompson started for the Reds but fared no better than veterans Derringer and Walters, who had lost games one and two. Thompson gave up just five hits in his four and two-thirds innings, but four of them were home runs and the Reds fell, 7-3.

Despite being down three games to none, game four on October 9 drew another crowd of over 32,000, and they watched the Reds take a 4-2 lead into the ninth inning. But the Reds then gave up the tying runs on an error and an infield single. That set the stage for the infamous tenth inning and Ernie Lombardi's "snooze" at home plate.

With the score still tied, and two on and one out, Dimaggio

Spectators filled the bleachers and sat atop the wall for game three of the 1939 World Series. As it had in the 1919 World series, Hulbert Hall, occupied by the the Young & Bertke Co. provided free window seats for dozens of fans.

singled to right driving in one run. But when Ival Goodman muffed the ball, Charlie Keller also tried to score and rammed into Lombardi at the plate. The collision left Lombardi in a lump and the ball rolled a few feet away. Seeing no one backing up the play, Dimaggio raced around third and headed for home. By the time Lombardi recovered, Dimaggio had slid across the plate with the third run, having circled the bases thanks to two errors, a dazed catcher, and Bucky Walter's failure to back up home plate.

The Reds, who had the best fielding team in the National League, had played like Knotholers. And Lombardi's prone position at the plate became the focus of the disaster for the sportswriters. Why, old Ernie decided to take a snooze while the Yankees ran the bases!

Years later Johnny Vander Meer came to his teammate's defense. "The ball came in on a bad hop and it hit Lom under the cup," said Vandy. "The ball absolutely paralyzed him." But Lom never spoke of the play and endured the public humiliation of the "snooze" label for years; the episode probably delayed his induction into the Hall of Fame.

In the locker room after the game, McKechnie did not dwell on the errors or the loss. He congratulated each player on the season and promised them they would be back in 1940. He was right. ◆

In the final game of the 1939 series at Crosley Field, a standing-room-only crowd of 32,794 watched the Reds lose a 4-2 ninth-inning lead. Joe Dimaggio had just singled to left field, sending Charlie Keller to third. Both would eventually score to tie the game. In the tenth, Keller collided with Ernie Lombardi at the plate, momentarily stunning the big catcher, who lay dazed at the plate with the ball just feet away while Dimaggio scored.

The large sign on the left field wall was baseball's logo celebrating the centennial of Abner Doubleday's "invention" of the game in 1839. The logo appeared on the wall all season.

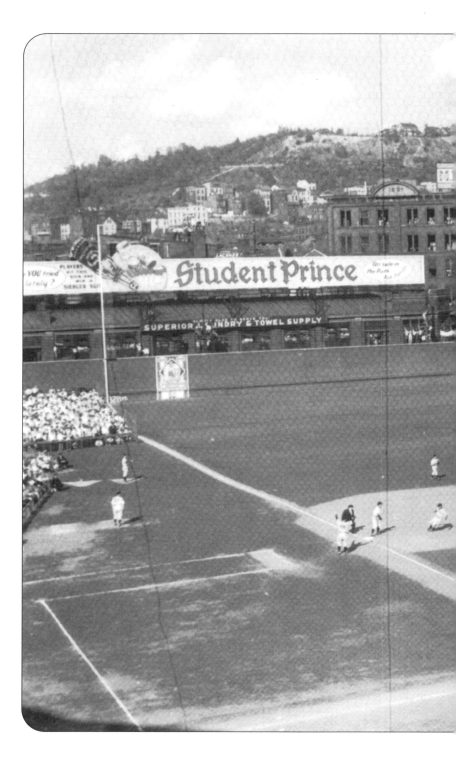

Crosley Field

The Sixth

1940-1949
Champions on the Eve of War

A FTER THE TUMULTOUS DECADE OF THE 1930S, THE FORTIES BROUGHT relative quiet to Crosley Field: no structural changes, no shifts in the playing field, no historic "firsts" of the magnitude of night baseball. Like the rest of the country, baseball in the 1940s reflected the great impact of World War II, and the evolution of the game slowed while the nation devoted its resources to winning the war.

But in the first year of the decade, the last year before America joined the war, Cincinnatians enjoyed the pleasures of a World Championship. For a brief interlude in October 1940, the Reds knocked world events off the front pages of the local papers, and Crosley Field rocked with cheers for a World Series winner.

The second largest Opening Day crowd in Crosley's history, 34,342, filled the park on April 16 to salute the 1939 National League champions and watch the Reds beat the Cubs, 2-1. The close score was a margin fans came to appreciate over the season as the Reds specialized in one-run victories. Their excellent pitching, strengthened by the addition of relief specialist Joe Beggs, and strong defense kept the Reds in almost every game.

On April 23, Crosley Field was the site of the first postponement in major league history due to a flood. Flood water from the Millcreek backed up into the ballpark through drains, and although the river levels were far below the historic 1937 flood, once the flood stage reached 57 feet, the water began to pool on the field and two games against the Cardinals had to be postponed.

The Reds battled the Dodgers for first place and took the lead for good on July 7. They appeared to have an insurmountable lead of nine games by late July when tragedy struck. Reserve catcher Willard Hershberger cut his throat with a razor in Boston on August 3. Hershberger had been despondent over a recent loss to the Giants; he blamed himself for calling the wrong pitches that resulted in two ninth-inning home runs. But other demons had also stalked "Hershey." In the weeks preceding the suicide, two of his teammates had heard

Commissioner K.M. Landis (left) congratulated Reds General Manager Warren Giles (right) and manager Bill McKechnie on Cincinnati's 1940 World Series win.

him threaten to end his life. Yet his death came as a shock to the club, and to all of baseball. Nothing similar had ever happened during a season.

When the Reds returned to Crosley Field on August 8, the club held a brief ceremony prior to the game. As the center field flag was lowered to half-mast, and the field was cleared, a wreath of flowers was placed on home plate, and the fans observed a long moment of silence. Bob Littlejohn, an usher at Crosley in the 1930s and 1940s, remembers it as the saddest day he ever spent at the park.

The Reds eventually recovered from their grief and dedicated the season to Hershberger. In September, they ran off a string of victories for a total of 100, the first Reds team ever to win a 100 games.

The club prepared Crosley Field for its second straight World Series, and the Reds only had to watch the scoreboard to see if their opponents would be the Indians, Yankees, or the Tigers. The hard-hitting Tigers finally edged the Indians by one game and the 1940 series was set. ◆

The Reds raised the National League championship banner – designed by a Cincinnati woman in a contest – on May 26, 1940, while the visiting St. Louis Cardinals looked on. Willard Hershberger, who would take his life just ten weeks after this flag-raising, was sixth from the left. Other Reds, from the left, included: Bill Werber, Lonnie Frey, Ival Goodman, Frank McCormick, Ernie Lombardi, and Hershberger. From the right were manager McKechnie, coach and later substitute catcher Jimmy Wilson, Bucky Walters, coach Hank Gowdy, Paul Derringer, Gene Thompson, an unidentified player, and Johnny Vander Meer

Bucky and Oom Paul

They were Cincinnati's version of "Me and Paul," the moniker made famous a decade earlier by Dizzy Dean and his brother. But the only thing the St. Louis Cardinals' pitchers had on the Cincinnati Reds' Bucky Walters and Paul Derringer was relative.

Bucky, 30, a sinker-balling former third baseman with an easy smile, and Paul, 33, a high-rolling Kentuckian with million-dollar control and style to match, won 52 games and a pennant in 1939. In 1940, they won 42 games, and four more in the World Series.

Derringer was emotional, outgoing. ("When are you bastards going to get me a run?" he would ask his teammates in the dugout.) Walters was cooler, quieter. Derringer rarely pitched low-hit games, but was money in the bank when the game was on the line. Walters was always "on," never careless. Derringer had a high leg kick; Walters was pure efficiency. Opposites in personality, they were birds of a feather professionally.

The Reds have never had a 1-2 starting punch that has come even close.

"Duke was a big, impressive guy," said Walters of Derringer. "He dressed well, ate well, and traveled first class all the way. Cocky? Yeah. But are you cocky if you can back it up?"

Derringer, in turn, admired Walters all-around play. It was nothing for Bucky to get six or eight assists in a game. He also swung a potent bat. He hit .325 in 1939; in his game six victory in the 1940 World Series, he pitched a shutout (4-0) and hit a homer. Oh how Derringer would have loved to do that.

Bucky threw a natural sinker, which ran in on right-handed hitters. In Bucky's early days as a Phillies' pitcher struggling against left-handed hitters ("they'd slap the low-and-away sinker to left," said Walters), former pitching great Albert "Chief"

Bender, a Chippewa Indian who would later be inducted into Cooperstown, pulled the young man aside.

"I had this little pitch that would break in sharply on left-handers' fists," Bender told Walters. "Why don't you try it?" For Walters, it was like Squanto giving the Pilgrims a handful of seed corn. "What it was, was a slider," said Walters. "Chief was throwing it in 1900....I had to be pretty exact with it, but it'd break just enough to jam left-handers. It's just what I needed."

Derringer's arsenal was more varied – screwballs from three different angles, several fastballs, and a "mystery" pitch.

"If I got a rough ball, I'd throw it out," said Walters. "Old Duke wouldn't. He was fond of saying, 'Let's leave a little mystery in the game.'" Part of the mystery was a well-disguised spitball that Derringer would break out in tough situations for demons like Johnny Mize. But "Oom Paul" never abused the pitch and his control numbers reflect it: in 1939 he walked only 35 hitters in 301 innings, and 12 of those were intentional.

"Duke," "Oom Paul." Derringer collected nicknames. "We didn't call him 'Duke' for nothing," said former teammate Johnny Vander Meer. "Paul had a regal bearing on the mound and off of it. He was a big operator."

"We'd hear rumors about some of his escapades across the river in Kentucky," said former teammate Harry Craft. The next day they'd see Duke motion for coach Hank Gowdy, and then they'd watch the big pitcher chase fungoes in the outfield, sweating out the whiskey. "He was a horse," said Walters. "He never missed a turn."

"Oom Paul" came from Frank Grayson of the *Times-Star* in 1933. "Oom Paul Kruger was the president of South African Boer

Republic and the old gentleman was in there pitching against the British every minute in their martial fracas," wrote Grayson. "The word 'Oom,' which means uncle or something like it, sounded so sonorous that we hung it on the big pitcher just to see what would happen…and he can't get (rid) of it."

Derringer was born in Springfield, Kentucky, 110 miles southwest of Cincinnati. In between farm chores, the barrel-chested youngster played catcher on the local teams. When plowing, he first gained an appreciation for the art of control. Instead of yelling "gee" and "haw" at the mule in front of him, he threw clods of dirt at its left and right ears.

Walters developed his pitching arm at third base, the position he first played. But in 1934, Phillies manager Jimmie Wilson suggested that his strong-armed infielder pitch the last couple of games of the season. By 1937, Walters was an All-Star pitcher. When Bill McKechnie was named manager of the Reds in 1938, he brought along Wilson, who pushed for the Reds to get Walters. Bucky led the Reds and the league in victories (27) in 1939, and was named MVP.

"Oh how I hate to come to Cincinnati," said a New York sportswriter in 1939. "One day you look at Walters (left). The next day its Derringer (right). On the third day you think you're going to win and Frank McCormick or Ival Goodman beats your brains out. Then it's…Walters and Derringer again."

Walters was a big-game pitcher, but Derringer had presaged Walters in the aura department. In 1939, Oom Paul won the Reds' nail-biting pennant-clincher, finishing it by striking out Joe Medwick and Johnny Mize. When Reds manager Bill McKechnie was asked who would pitch the seventh game of the 1940 World Series at Crosley Field, he didn't hesitate.

"Big Paul," said McKechnie. "It will be Big Paul today, tomorrow, or any day the final game is played." Derringer won, 2-1, gutting out yet another white-knuckler.

Nobody's smile beamed brighter than Bucky's. ◆

Victory in Seven

Though the Reds dominated the National League, and were early favorites to defeat the Tigers, injuries to Ernie Lombardi and second baseman Lonnie Frey cast a big shadow over the Reds' hopes. Lombardi had sprained an ankle in mid-September, and with Hershberger's death, the Reds desperately needed an experienced reserve catcher. McKechnie activated his 40-year-old coach Jimmy Wilson, who had been an excellent catcher in his playing days. He handled the duties for 16 games in September, and when Lombardi's ankle failed to respond, Wilson became the surprise starter for the series. Then, just five days before the series opened, Frey dropped a iron lid off the dugout water cooler on his foot, and steady reserve Eddie Joost replaced him.

Despite the loss of the two starters, Cincinnatians filled Crosley Field for the opening game on October 2. The series promised to be a close duel between the heavy-hitting Tigers, who had lead the American League in runs scored, and the defensive-minded Reds who had led the National League in pitching and fielding. For the second straight October, Crosley Field

The 1940 regulars posed in the Reds dugout prior to the start of the 1940 World Series: (from left) Bill Werber, Mike McCormick, Ival Goodman, Frank McCormick, Jimmy Ripple, Ernie Lombardi, Eddie Joost, Billy Myers, and Lonnie Frey.

Movie camera operators shared the roof of Crosley Field with local radio stations, including WKRC. The temporary expanded press box, visible in the background, hosted over 80 Western Union telegraph operators, dozens of out-of-town reporters, and a broadcast team from radio station CMCQ in Cuba. According to the Enquirer, *"The whole island has been rooting for the Reds since spring training when McKechnie's boys took a four-day jaunt to Havana to play the Cuban All-Stars."*

wore red, white, and blue bunting both inside and outside the park. The festivities at Findlay and Western began the night of October 1 as hundreds of fans lined up at the ticket windows. They were joined by thousands more in the morning eager to purchase bleacher seats or standing-room-only tickets at $3.45 for the first game. Tiger Pitcher Bobo Newsom beat Derringer, 7-2, in the first game, but Bucky Walters pitched the Reds to a 5-3 victory the next day.

In Detroit, the Tigers took two games out of three and the series returned to Crosley Field on October 7 with the Reds trailing three games to two. But McKechnie wasn't worried. "I've got Walters and Derringer to shoot at 'em," he said. Walters took care of his win in game six with a 4-0 win. Now it was up to Derringer.

Amazingly, the game was not a sell-out, only 26,854 in the park, some 3,500 short of capacity. However, in this era, tickets to games six and seven of a World Series were not sold as part of a package in advance. They were only sold as the need arose, and so tickets for game seven did not go on sale until the Reds won game six. All 26,854 tickets were sold in just 24 hours. Despite the

Crosley Field

availability of seats, the windows of the factories overlooking the park were well filled. Through field glasses, one reporter observed "spectators packed into every vantage point across the street from the ball park....Three men were atop a high tension electric pole, while still farther away a group of a dozen were propped on a steep roof...."

Whether the fans were inside or outside the park, they saw one of the great games in the history of Crosley Field, and with their loud support, actually contributed to the winning rally. The Tigers led, 1-0, going into the bottom of the seventh. Frank McCormick led off the inning with a long drive to left. Tiger left fielder Hank Greenberg may have had a chance at the ball, but stumbled on the terrace and McCormick had a double.

Jimmy Ripple then hit a double to deep right field, but McCormick held up thinking the ball would be caught, and got a late start for home. Shortstop Dick Bartell grabbed the relay throw in time to make a play at the plate. But with his back to the infield, and with the crowd making a awful racket, Bartell failed to hear his teammates shouting for him to throw home, and McCormick scored the tying run.

Ripple was sacrificed to third and after pinch-hitter Lombardi was walked intentionally, the light-hitting Billy Meyers drove a long fly to center. Ripple tagged up and scored easily with what proved to be the winning run. Derringer gave up two hard hit balls in the eighth, but got out of the inning, and retired the Tigers one-two-three in the ninth, and for the only time in Crosley's history, the Reds won the deciding game of a World Series at home.   ◆

The winning run in the game seven of the 1940 series scored just seconds after this picture was taken. Billy Meyers had just hit a long drive to center field. As manager McKechnie (1) shouted instructions, Jimmy Ripple (22) ran back to third base, tagged up on the catch, and scored the winning run. Bobo Newsom, whose father died of a heart attack during the World Series, pitched for Detroit.

Note the empty seats in the right field grandstands. The crowd for game seven was 3,500 below capacity.

Below: *The Reds mobbed Paul Derringer after the final out of the 1940 World Series. Soon after, youngsters jumped out of the stands and ran about the outfield, and delirious fans tossed hundreds of cushions from the grandstands onto the field. Downtown, work stopped, ticker tape cascaded from office windows, and people, automobiles and streetcars combined to create a celebration not seen since the end of WWI.*

Right: *In the Reds locker room, Jimmy Wilson (with the soft drink) and Mike McCormick hoisted Derringer, who shook hands with general manager Warren Giles. A happy Bucky Walters cheered behind Giles. Jimmy Ripple (not pictured) stood in his birthday suit, beer in one hand and cigarette in the other and repeated, "We're the World's Champions, the blankety blank champs. Boy, that sounds good."*

Crosley Field

War and Baseball

"Wartime Opening Proves Solemn Affair," headlined the *Enquirer* above its story of Opening Day, 1942. America had entered World War II just four months earlier and events at Crosley Field over the next four seasons would reflect the country's ever-increasing involvement and sacrifices.

Although the game itself on April 14, 1942, appeared no different than others, the opening ceremonies received particular attention. "There was no haphazard jostling or muffled talking," during the flag ceremonies, reported the *Enquirer*. The men held their hats reverently over their hearts and stood in an erect military fashion.

Major leagues played baseball throughout the war, given the go-ahead by President Franklin D. Roosevelt. Some 500 major league players were drafted, however, and most teams were forced to sign over-aged veterans and immature rookies to fill out the rosters. The attendance at Crosley Field dropped with the quality of play. The Reds drew 643,000 in 1941 and fell to 290,000 by 1945.

Travel to the ballpark, like travel everywhere else was restricted by gas rationing. The Office of Price Administration warned fans on the eve of Opening Day, 1943, that use of taxicabs to go to Crosley Field would violate rationing regulations. Travel by streetcar or bus was within the regulations, but the transit company was not permitted to add extra cars or buses as it normally would for Opening Day. Restrictions on train travel and automobile miles meant that most out-of-town fans stayed home.

The Reds also cut back on regular travel accommodations. The club announced in 1942 that the team would travel in two Pullman cars instead of three. This required six to eight players to sleep in upper berths, which had previously been left vacant. But Lou Smith, the *Enquirer* baseball writer noted the boys weren't complaining. "Compared to the fox holes of the Phillipines sleeping in uppers isn't exactly a hardship."

To further save travel expenses, the Reds abandoned their Florida spring training site for 1943, '44, and '45 and trained at Indiana University in Bloomington.

The club held special promotions geared to the war effort. All service men, and kids under 18 who collected 100 pounds of scrap paper were admitted free. In 1942 and 1943, the Reds combined a regular game with an exhibition game against the Great Lakes Naval Training team in a twi-night doubleheader. In '42, the Reds and their regular opponents, the Cubs, combined squads for an "all-star" exhibition lineup to play the Naval team, and then played their regular game afterwards. All proceeds benefitted the Army-Navy relief fund.

The work schedules of most families were altered by the war, with women joining the labor force in significant numbers, and with many factories scheduling additional shifts. In 1943, the club polled fans to see if changing the starting time of games would make it easier for fans to come to Crosley. Thirty-one percent voted for late morning starts, 25 percent for mid-afternoon, and 22 percent for late afternoon starts. In 1943 and 1944, the club experimented with an 11 a.m. starting time for some weekday games, but attendance did not noticeably improve.

The custom of keeping foul balls also bowed to the war effort. The club asked fans to return foul balls to ushers, who deposited them in a hopper next to the screen behind home plate. The balls were then sent to service men in the U.S. and overseas. ◆

Opening Day 1944 drew 30,154, about 1,000 over seating capacity. Unlike the pre-war years, however, there were no temporary seats placed in the outfield.

Representatives from the services participated in the flag presentation ceremonies, and a group of 500 soldiers had seats in a special section in left field.

The sign in deep right field admonished the crowd not to throw cushions, and also reminded fans that "all baseballs returned from stands will be sent to men in the service."

In the mid-1940s, the club painted a quote from former President Herbert Hoover on this wall: "Next to religion, baseball has furnished a greater impact on American life than any other institution."

Crosley Field

War Baby

"Warm up, Joe," said Reds manager Bill McKechnie.

Joe Nuxhall wasn't listening. He heard the words all right, but they didn't register. The words weren't for him. Couldn't be for him. No big-league manager would ever say words like that to a 15-year-old. Not even one dressed in a Reds uniform.

"There hadn't been any talk of me pitching in a game," Nuxhall recalled. "It was just, 'C'mon down to the game and sit on the bench.'" And that's what he was doing, this June 10, 1944, watching the Cardinals drub the Reds, 13-0.

The Reds, who were decimated like almost every other team by the exodus of players to the service in World War II, had been scouting Nuxhall since he was 14. Two months shy of his 16th birthday, Nuxhall was built like a man (6-foot-1, 190 pounds). Better, he threw hard, in the mid-80s. In his tryout before McKechnie, Nuxhall had thrown nothing but strikes and "really popped the mitt." In the summer of '43, he had dominated batters in the eight-team Hamilton Sunday Baseball League, where most of the players were in their mid-30s, like Nuxhall's dad, Orville. It was nothing for Little Nux to strike out 10-12 hitters in a nine-inning game, using nothing but fastballs.

Initially, the Reds scouts had come to watch Orville, a hard-throwing right-hander. But the best the scouts could offer him was a minor-league contract for a Class C team in Ogden, Utah. It wasn't enough money. There were five Nuxhall children to feed; Joe was the oldest.

Forget the old man, figured the Reds. Sign the kid. The kid might be able to put some people in the seats. *Come see the boy wonder from Hamilton try to throw the ball by Stan the Man*. You could make a promotion out of that.

Joe had been riding down to Cincinnati on a bus on nights and weekends. The bus let him off at Brighton Corner, six blocks from Crosley Field. He walked the rest of the way. At first he had dreams, day and night, about getting called into a game. But then, after seeing opportunity after opportunity pass, he came to believe it was a charade.

He went back to admiring the line drives explode off the bats of the Cardinals. Led by the great Stan Musial, the Cards were going for a third straight National League pennant.

"Joe, warm up!"

McKechnie yelled a little louder this time. Loud enough, anyway, to snap Nuxhall from his reverie. He looked up the bench at McKechnie.

"One second, you're admiring the scenery," Nuxhall would later say, "and the next second you're being told to get in the game. Kind of changes the thinking a little bit."

Nuxhall reached for his glove and clamored up the dugout steps. He almost made it. Suddenly, he smelled dirt. He was face down in front of the Reds dugout. He had tripped on the top step. The fans in the box seats guffawed. His teammates, some almost three times his age, laughed behind their hands. Nuxhall felt the blood rush to his head, and felt his face turn the same crimson hue as his hat. He gathered his glove and jogged to the bullpen, carefully placing one foot in front of the other. Once there, every fourth or fifth pitch he threw sailed wildly by the bullpen catcher. He couldn't help himself. "What am I going to do when I get in the game?" Nuxhall wondered.

Somehow, he threw strikes. He grounded out George Fallon, walked pitcher Mort Cooper, then popped up Augie Bergamo. Two outs. In stepped Debs Garms. Two quick strikes. Then Nuxhall caught a glimpse of Stan Musial in the on-deck circle.

"I began thinking, 'Geez, three weeks ago I was pitching in school against 12-, 13- and 14-year-olds,'" recalled Nuxhall. "Now here's Stan Musial in the on-deck circle. *Ball one, ball two, ball three, ball four.* I walked Garms and all hell broke loose."

Stanley Frank Musial. Stan the Man. Coiled, corkscrew stance. "6" on his back, plainly visible to Nuxhall on the mound.

"I would have thrown him a curve," said Nuxhall.

Why didn't he?

"I didn't have a curve. All l had was a fastball."

And Musial knew it.

"The thing that amazed me," Nuxhall said, "is that the Cardinals were up 13-0, but Musial was standing up there like it was a needle-threader. Wham! He hit a rope to right, an absolute rocket. That one loosened my knees."

The runners circled the bases. Then, three walks and a single.

Nuxhall stood mesmerized.

He had surrendered five earned runs in two-thirds of an inning.

The Reds trailed, 18-0.

Epilogue: Eight years later, "Nuxie" worked his way back to the big leagues in 1952 and recorded that elusive third out — and quite a few more. He won 135 games in a 15-year career and lowered his 67.50 ERA to a creditable 3.90. Twice he made the National League All-Star team, and was elected to the Reds Hall of Fame. But he'll never forget that day that he became the youngest player in major-league history.

"My classmates couldn't believe that somebody in their ninth-grade class had pitched in a major-league game," said Nuxhall.

The youngest player ever, Hamilton's 15-year-old Joe Nuxhall, posed with manager Bill McKechnie on June 10, 1944. The Reds signed Nuxhall for $175 a month and a $500 bonus.

They may not have believed it, but they wanted to commemorate it. On June 10, 1994, Hamilton city leaders changed the name of Ford Boulevard to Joe Nuxhall Boulevard. It runs next to the diamonds where the Reds discovered a young lefthander playing summer ball in league with his dad. ◆

Crosley After the War

In the years following World War II, the players returned to baseball and so did the crowds. In 1945, just 290,000 visited Crosley Field to see a seventh-place club; in 1946, the Reds improved only to sixth place, but attendance jumped to 715,700.

The increase in attendance occurred despite a modest increase in ticket prices. Upper deck box seats, the most expensive, went from $2.00 to $2.20; unreserved grandstand went from $1.10 to $1.20 and bleacher seats jumped a nickel from 60 cents to 65 cents. At the concession stands, fans could still fill up on a dollar. Red hots were 15 cents, Coca-Cola a dime, peanuts a dime, and local beers cost 20 cents.

The Reds did not fare well in the standings in the late 1940s, never finishing above .500, but several milestones and record-setting performances made this a memorable time at Crosley Field. Just weeks after the war ended, on September 13, 1945, the smallest crowd in the history of Crosley, 281, watched the Reds lose to the Giants. The Reds were on their way to seventh place and their worst finish since 1937.

A little over a year later, on April 27, 1947, the largest crowd in the history of Crosley, 36,961, watched the Reds sweep the Pirates in a double header. Capacity was listed as 30,101, and with no additional seats on the field, some 6,860 standing room tickets were sold. It was an odd time to set a record, not an Opening Day, nor a World Series, nor a key game in a pennant race, but a routine Sunday double header early in the season.

Two notable individual achievements highlighted the late 1940s. From May 10 to July 25, 1947, Ewell Blackwell racked up 16 consecutive pitching victories without a loss, including a no-hitter. And on July 6, 1949, Reds outfielder Walker Cooper set the all-time club record with 10 RBIs in a game, including three home runs as the Reds killed the Cubs, 23-4.

There were few changes in the appearance of the park in the '40s. Prior to the 1946 season, the club moved the screen behind home plate 18 feet closer to the field, and installed new seats in front of the right field bleachers, reducing the right

On Opening Day, 1949, St. Louis catcher Del Rice tagged out Reds runner Virgil Stallcup. The wall in right field no longer carried war-related messages; it now listed the price of concessions.

field dimensions from 366 feet to 342 feet (see page 146). And, in 1947, the club removed pay phones from the park to cut down on betting.

Perhaps the most significant change at Crosley in the late 1940s was the arrival of television. The first telecast was a Reds-Cubs game September 21, 1947 over W8XCT, the predecessor to WLWT. WLW estimated the home audience at 10,000. Popular broadcaster Vernon "Red" Thornburgh called the game, which featured only two cameras, one behind first base and one behind home plate. Eventually, permanent roosts for cameras were mounted on the facade of the upper deck grandstand. By the mid-1950s, the Reds aired over 50 games a season. ◆

Opening Day of the 1949 season was telecast by WLW, and fans became accustomed to the new television camera platforms along the upper deck.

Baseball's Great Experiment Comes to Crosley

May 13, 1947. Crosley Field. The Cincinnati Reds vs. the Brooklyn Dodgers. Jackie Robinson's debut in Cincinnati.

There had been black ballplayers in this ballpark before, all the way back to 1920, when the Cincinnati Cuban Stars became the first Negro League club to lease a major-league ballpark. All the great black ballplayers had passed through the park at Findlay and Western. Negro League teams – the Cincinnati Tigers, Buckeyes and Clowns – had all played weekend games here in the 1930s and 1940s.

But this was different. This was a black ballplayer playing in Major League Baseball, previously the exclusive enclave of white Americans and a few light-skinned Latin-Americans.

Nobody knew what to expect. Two months earlier, even some of the Dodgers players had balked at the thought of playing on the same team as a black American. Alabamans Dixie Walker, Eddie Stanky, and Bobby Bragan, drew up a petition saying they would rather be traded than play with a black teammate. Kentuckian Pee Wee Reese, the Dodgers' shortstop, refused to sign. "If he can take my job," said Reese, "he's entitled to it." Dodger boss Branch Rickey ordered the rebellion stopped.

Cincinnati was the southern-most city in the major leagues, and in 1947 Cincinnati was still a segregated town. But on this warm Tuesday afternoon, 27,000 seats were filled. Reds pitcher Johnny Vander Meer remembered the day well. "A large portion of the crowd was black," recalled Ol' Double No-Hit. "It was a good sized crowd, a Saturday- or a Sunday-size crowd."

Many southern blacks filled the stands. "The train originated down in Birmingham, Alabama, that morning," recalled Vander Meer. "It got up the road, and they had to add another car. It got up the road some more, and they had to add another car. By the time it got to Cincinnati, they'd added an extra 10-12 cars."

Although Robinson had just one hit that day, "he was applauded every time he stepped to the plate," wrote *Cincinnati Enquirer* baseball reporter Lou Smith.

But later in the season, Robinson faced rude heckling in Cincinnati and brushback pitches from Ewell Blackwell. In 1951, Robinson received a death threat in the mail: "ROBINSON WE ARE GOING TO KILL YOU IF YOU ATTEMPT TO ENTER A BALL GAME AT CROSLEY FIELD." Robinson responded with a home run.

The cozy atmosphere of Crosley, much revered by the fans, worked against the black players. One of the first African-American players for the Giants, Hank Thompson, did not enjoy playing the Reds. Jules Tygiel in his book *Baseball's Great Experiment* quotes Thompson: "The worst fans were in Cincinnati. Whenever there was a lull, some loudmouth would yell: 'Nigger' or 'black unprintable' and you could hear it all over the place."

In 1954, the Reds became the seventh of eight National League teams to sign a black player: outfielder Chuck Harmon. By 1954 the taunts from the stands had diminished, and most of the players had come to accept an integrated lineup. "You know how cozy Crosley Field was," remembered Harmon. "You're right there next to people. You can hear anybody talk. But I can't remember anybody saying anything offensive to me."

Bob Thurman, another black outfielder who joined the Reds in 1955, fondly remembered his teammates, who included many Southerners. "That's the greatest set of guys you ever wanted to be around. They didn't think nothing about any color."

Things change. Even the National Pastime. Jackie Robinson had changed baseball. ◆

When the Dodgers visited Crosley Field in May 1947, Jackie Robinson was the starting first baseman. Here, Robinson has just tagged out Reds shortstop Eddie Miller. Umpire Babe Pinelli made the call.

This photo was taken in Robinson's second game in Cincinnati. Blacks turned out to support Robinson on this day. Lou Smith of the Enquirer estimated that half of the 6,607 fans in the ballpark were black.

The "Whip"

The Whip. Sidewinder. Blackie.

Those were some of Ewell Blackwell's nicknames. He stood 6-foot-6 and weighed 195 pounds. Sportswriter Red Smith once described him as a "fly rod with ears."

Right-handed hitters had other names for him.

He had a wicked, right-handed sidearm delivery which caused his fastball to run in, and down, on right-handed hitters.

"Off the field he was the nicest guy in the world," said Hank Sauer, a former Red who was later traded to the Cubs and faced Blackwell often. "On the field, he was a competitor. Everybody was intimidated by him."

Blackwell played for the Reds in 1942 and from 1946 to 1952. l947 was his year. He won 16 straight games in a row, starting and finishing every one of them. He led the National League in strikeouts, complete games and victories (22-6). He threw six shutouts and had a 2.47 ERA. He almost duplicated Johnny Vander Meer's back-to-back no-hitters of nine years earlier. Blackwell no-hit the Boston Braves at Crosley Field on June 18, and was two outs away from another no-hitter four days later at Crosley Field when Eddie Stanky slapped a single between Blackwell's legs.

"Of every 10 pitches I threw, nine were fastballs," Blackwell said. "I was clocked at 99.8 mph….Bob Feller had identical time. I was always wild. I didn't walk too many batters, but I would lead the league six times in hit batters….I realized my sidearm delivery was intimidating, and I took advantage of it any way I could."

Blackwell's delivery came naturally to him. His high school coach outside Los Angeles in the late 1930s tried in vain to get Blackwell to throw over the top. Even when he played shortstop, Blackwell threw sidearm.

"On Sundays, I pitched semipro ball," Blackwell said. "I was a shy kid, but on the field I was a different person."

He received nine offers from pro scouts, but signed with the Reds in December, 1941, because they promised to send him to big-league spring training in 1942. "Dad figured that if I was sent to the minors, nobody would hear from me again," said Blackwell.

Nineteen years old, he went north with the big club that April. He was surrounded by veteran pitchers like Paul Derringer and Bucky Walters. Ultimately, the Reds sent him down to Syracuse for seasoning. That's when World War II intervened and Blackwell didn't see the majors again until 1946, when he filled the rotation slot of the retired Derringer.

Blackwell's pitching philosophy was simple. "I owned three-quarters of the plate," he said. "I didn't try to hit anyone."

He could have fooled slugger Ralph Kiner.

"Ewell Blackwell was a scary pitcher because he was mean and would throw at you anytime," said Kiner. "Your legs shook when you tried to dig in on him because of that sidearm delivery."

After his great season in 1947, Blackwell injured his shoulder in an exhibition game in Columbia, South Carolina, in late March, 1948, on a cold, windy rainy day. His arm never recovered. He won only seven games that season. By 1952, Blackwell had been traded to the New York Yankees.

"My years in Cincinnati had been wonderful," he said. "It was a great, friendly town….My wife went to almost all the games and sat with the wives of other players....There was tremendous camaraderie among the players." He fondly recalled the old ballyard at Findlay and Western. "I even liked pitching at Crosley," he said, "even though it was the smallest park in the league."

But it was never so small as when "The Whip" was on the mound. For hitters, he made the place downright claustrophobic. ◆

Ewell Blackwell posed with his fiancee in 1948. Blackwell was chosen for six All-Star games, which ties him with Paul Derringer for most selections by a Cincinnati pitcher. In his last five All-Star appearances, Blackwell pitched 11 shutout innings, with one win and one save.

The Seventh

1950-1959: Glory Days

"Big Klu," Ted Kluszewski was the most popular Redleg of the 1950s. He was the starting first baseman from 1948 through 1956 and hit a then-club record 49 home runs in 1954.

THERE WERE NO CINCINNATI PENNANTS WON IN THE 1950S NOR WORLD Series played – in fact the team only had two winning seasons – but many who remember Crosley Field consider the '50s to be the ballpark's golden era. By the end of the decade, parking nightmares and questions about the future of Crosley Field had surfaced, but for most, the '50s harken memories of Klu, Robby, the Sun Deck and Moon Deck, and the "Goat Run."

By the 1960s, the ambience of Crosley Field had changed, the surrounding neighborhood demolished for additional parking and I-75. The game itself was undergoing a radical shift with franchise moves, expansion, and plans for new super stadiums (with plastic grass). The '50s, then, were a watershed era in baseball, and the last hurrah for old parks like Crosley.

There were plenty of hurrahs at Findlay and Western as the Reds – or Redlegs as they were officially known from 1954 to 1958 – drew nearly seven and one-half million fans in ten seasons, a million more than ever before. The Reds began the '50s in the middle of a ten-year second division slump, and attendance in 1950 was the lowest of the decade, 539,000, or about 7,100 per game. But the fabled home run club of 1956 which contended for the pennant until the final week of the season, drew 1,125,928, the first time in the history of Crosley Field that attendance hit the million mark, and the all-time single-season attendance record for Crosley.

Ticket prices rose very little in the 1950s. In 1959, all box seats were $2.50, grandstand general admission was $1.50, and Sun Deck seats were 75 cents.

The change in the team name was a victim of the Cold War standoff between the "Reds" of the Soviet Union and the "Yanks" of the United States. Major League baseball urged the Cincinnati club to change the team name to something more patriotic and the Cincinnati Reds became the Redlegs. However, owner Powel Crosley never liked the change, and the team and the public used Redlegs and Reds interchangeably. ◆

This aerial photograph captured an Opening Day crowd from the mid-1950s, perhaps 1955 as the outfield signs match the photo on pages 128-29. The capacity of the ballpark in the 1950s ranged from a low of 29,439 in 1953 to 30,322 in 1959. In 1950, the club added a press box elevator, housed in the white tower at the rear of the main grandstand.

The Governor and the Mayor frequently appeared at Opening Day, and attendance usually topped 30,000. As was customary, the club seated the overflow on the outfield terraces. Despite the civic enthusiasm, the Reds lost eight of ten openers in the '50s, the only victories belonging to Joe Nuxhall (1954) and Bob Purkey (1959).

Crosley Field

Left: *A new voice became part of the familiar Crosley sounds of the 1950s. Paul Sommerkamp (shown here during a rain delay in the mid-1960s) took over the public address announcer's job in 1951, and conducted business from his seat adjacent to the visitors' dugout. Despite illness and the occasionally nasty weather conditions that swept through Cincinnati, Sommerkamp never missed one game at Crosley Field. He continued his public address chores at Riverfront Stadium, and retired in 1985. Sommerkamp developed a unique style of introducing the players by repeating the last name. "Batting first, Pete Rose......Rose."*

Right: *In 1958, the fans left Crosley Field after the Reds dropped the opener, 5-4, to the Phillies. Many headed to the trolleys that lined Dalton Avenue. On Opening Days the city placed extra trolleys and buses in service to handle the big crowds.*

This view looked south, from the upper deck of the right field stands down Dalton Street past the Post Office towards Cincinnati Union Terminal.

Crosley Field

Crosley Field

The Chicago Cubs scored the first runs of the Opening Day game of 1955 on a double by Dee Fondy into the left-field terrace seats, and went on to down the Redlegs, 7-5. One Hall of Famer was on the field: Cubs shortstop Ernie Banks, who raced around third with the second run.

The Redlegs starting line up included Johnny Temple (2b), Roy McMillan (ss), Gus Bell (cf), Ted Kluszewski (1b), Ray Jablonski (3b), Jim Greengrass (lf), Ed Bailey (c), Wally Post (rf), and Art Fowler (p). Joe Nuxhall appeared in relief. The attendance was 33,195.

Crosley's familiar neighborhood landmarks, some dating from the construction of the park in 1912, were almost a part of the park itself, including the factory buildings behind the center field wall and the right field bleachers. The laundry was just out of view to the left. The signs advertised popular Cincinnati attractions and businesses from the 1950s including Coney Island and Shillito's department stores. The Young and Bertke Company's sign, with the animated figure, became a landmark of the 1940s, '50s and '60s.

Among Crosley's idiosyncrasies were the ground rules painted on the outfield fence from the late 1940s to the mid-1960s. Visible in right center field was the rule: "Batted ball hitting wall to right of white line on fly home run." A second ground rule, just to the right of the scoreboard, but hidden by the crowd, read: "Batted ball remaining back of barrier 2 base hit Bouncing out—in play." Crosley Field was the only major league park to have ground rules written on the outfield walls.

Big Klu

What Clark Gable did for the sleeveless T-shirt, Ted Kluszewski couldn't do for the sleeveless baseball uniform.

Set a fashion trend.

Nobody could wear a baseball uniform like Big Klu.

Kluszewski, the son of Polish immigrants, was as feared a slugger as there was in baseball from 1953 through 1955, when he rattled 40, 49, and 47 home runs for the Cincinnati Reds. But it is the why he did it, the way he *looked*, which he will forever be remembered.

"We had those flannel uniforms, and every time I'd swing, it would get hung up on the sleeve," said Klu, referring to the tightness of the sleeve around his massive upper arms. "I complained about it, but they (the Reds front office) hemmed and hawed and finally I took a pair of scissors and cut them off. They got pretty upset, but it was either that or change my swing. And I wasn't going to change my swing."

In 1954, Klu's 49 home runs (34 of them at Crosley) and 141 RBI (.326 batting average) led the National League. Among the other "greats" in their prime that year were Duke Snider, Eddie Mathews, Gil Hodges, Willie Mays and Stan Musial.

"I think '54 had more of the great names than any other time I can remember," said Klu. "It really was the golden age of baseball."

Klu was born and raised in Argo, Illinois, where Ted and his brother, John, worked at the cornstarch plant, loading 140-pound bags onto trucks during the summertime. ("That's where he got his big arms," said John.) Ted played two seasons of high school baseball but preferred football. Upon graduating, he went to work full-time at the cornstarch plant, to try to save enough money to marry his high school sweetheart, 5-foot-2 Eleanor Guckel, a softball pitcher. Klu had no money for college, and no time for baseball. His parents were sick. (They died before Klu, one of their six children, made the major leagues.)

"After a hard day at the factory, it would have been no fun to catch a local into Chicago to play twilight ball," explained Klu. He played "prairie football," a wide-open form of the sport popular in and around Chicago, however. It was there he caught the attention of a semipro official, who notified Indiana University, which offered a scholarship. As a sophomore, tight end Klu was "All Big Nine" conference and an honorable mention All-America. He caught the winning pass over Michigan which gave IU the conference title. Once he caught three touchdowns on successive plays against Illinois. The first was nullified because his foot was over the back line of the end zone. The second was nullified because an official had called time out when a Dalmatian walked onto the field. The third counted. IU won, 7-0.

The Reds "discovered" Klu in March 1945. Wartime travel restrictions precluded the Reds from training in Tampa, so they worked out in Bloomington, Indiana, home of IU. Ted, who had gone out for IU's baseball team as a way of avoiding the boring rigors of spring football, took the diamond with his teammates after the Reds were done for the day. Reds' groundskeeper Lenny Schwab noticed that Klu's drives were clearing a center field embankment, something none of the Reds hitters could do. Manager Bill McKechnie talked to the IU football coach; a year later, Klu had a big bonus, a wife, and a promising career. But it would take him two years to get rid of his "football shoulders," a muscular tightness which interfered with the freedom and rhythm of his swing. At Crosley Field, Klu's wife took film of him at bat. Together, they studied it.

"The movies showed I was falling away with my shoulders," explained Klu. "I thought my fault was overstriding. As soon as we ran the movies, I was able to correct my mistake."

Although Klu hit many of his 259 homers to right field at Crosley, he retained that "straightaway power" that made the Reds first take notice. Even the customers at the Scoreboard Cafe,

This classic Crosley Field view was taken on September 22, 1955, Ted Kluszewski at bat against Milwaukee pitcher Phil Paine. Klu did not homer on this swing, but in the sixth inning, Klu hit his 47th and final home run of the season.

The big Redleg star on this day, however, was Gus Bell, who drove in eight RBI with a home run, a double, and two singles. The four-run first on the scoreboard for the Reds was courtesy of a Bell grand slam. The Reds eventually won, 15-4; Johnny Klippstein picked up his ninth win.

The Siebler "hit-this-sign-and-win-a-free-suit" sign is visible at the right edge of the Bavarian Beer sign atop the laundry. Just 1,503 enjoyed the afternoon slugfest at Crosley Field.

Crosley Field

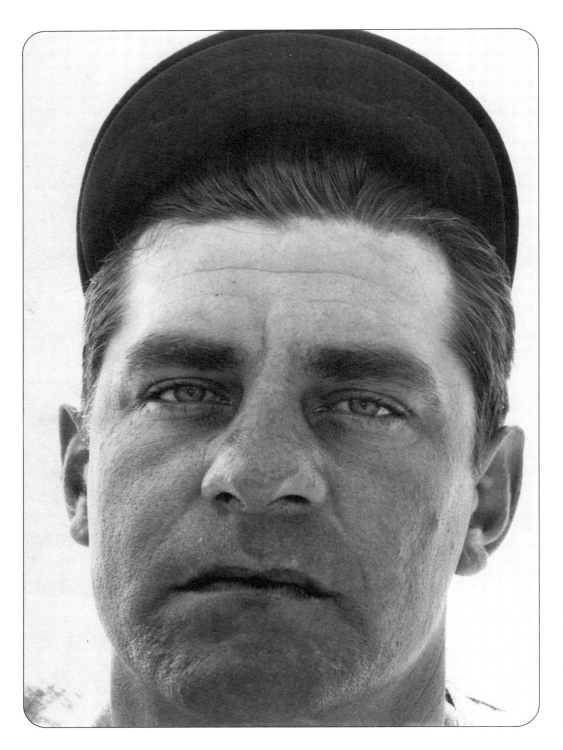

Ted Kluszewski was the Reds starting first baseman from 1948 to 1956. He developed back problems at age 32 in 1957 and the Reds traded him to Pittsburgh in 1958. When he retired he held the club career records for home runs and RBI. Klu returned to the Reds as a hitting instructor.

located across the street from Crosley's center field wall, looked over their shoulders instinctively when WKRC's Waite Hoyt announced that Big Klu was coming to the plate.

Klu never lost all of the football player in him. Reds right fielder Mike McCormick got a taste of Big Klu's running power in spring training 1946 when he and Klu were chasing a pop fly in short right. Klu, oblivious to McCormick's hard-charging presence, caught the ball and flattened McCormick. Klu's momentum carried him past McCormick, but Klu backtracked to see what the hubbub was about. Other Reds had already gathered around their fallen right fielder.

"What happened?" asked Klu.

"What happened?" retorted a teammate, incredulously. "You almost killed McCormick!"

"I'm sorry, Mike," said Klu, sheepishly. "I thought I just brushed you."

"If what you did is 'brush' me," said McCormick, "I'd hate to meet you head-on."

Klu was no brute. He was a gentle, fun-loving, thinking man's ballplayer.

"Everybody loved Klu," said Reds pitcher Art Fowler. "I'd be agitating him and he'd grab me by the head and lead me around the clubhouse. I couldn't get loose from him because he was as strong as Hercules. He wouldn't fight because he was afraid he'd hurt someone."

Baseball writer Ritter Collett tells of the time there was an on-field scuffle at Crosley between the Reds and Cardinals. Solly Hemus was headed for the battle when, suddenly, he found himself suspended a foot off the ground.

"Where you going, Solly?" asked Klu, softly.

"Nowhere, Ted," said Solly, meekly.

Giants' star Willie Mays was fond of scooping up sand and putting it in Klu's back pocket upon reaching first base. One day, as Mays got ready to steal second base at Crosley, Klu stepped on his toes. Willie told the ump. But when the ump wasn't looking, Klu stepped on his toes again. Willie didn't steal any bases that day.

Klu loved a good joke, and sometimes he'd laugh so hard his eyes watered. He'd hide his eyes behind a handkerchief until the tears had mostly dried.

Earl Lawson, the veteran baseball scribe, tells of the time Klu was leaving a movie theatre in Knoxville, Tennessee. Klu had gone there with some of his Reds teammates, after an exhibition game in Knoxville had been rained out. Kluszewski thought he spotted Reds pitcher Harry Perkowski, who had a nose like Jimmy Durante's, sitting in an aisle seat. On the way by, Kluszewski gave Perkowski's proboscis a wiggle and loudly bellowed, "Honk! Honk!"

Upon returning to the team hotel, Klu was shocked when Perkowski greeted him in the lobby. "Harry, weren't you just in the theater?" Klu asked.

"Been here in the lobby all afternoon," answered Perkowski. Klu was dumfounded.

So, too, no doubt, was the man in the movie theatre.

Klu was a classic. His human qualities are what endeared him to his teammates, but his superhuman attributes are what most impressed everybody else.

When Leo Durocher left Klu's name off a list of baseball's strongest players, a writer asked: "What about Kluszewski?"

"Kluszewski?" huffed Durocher. "I'm talking about human beings."

Which is also pretty much why National League umpire Larry Goetz, a Cincinnati native, had to re-evaluate the opinion he formed one day while watching Ted Williams and Ralph Kiner in a home-run hitting contest before an exhibition game between the Boston Red Sox and Pittsburgh Pirates. Somebody remarked that if the ball was manufactured any livelier, it would only be a matter of time before a pitcher would be killed by a line drive batted through the box.

"I was pretty well-convinced there was such a possibility," said Goetz, "until a week later, when I was working a game in Cincinnati. This big Kluszewski comes up for the Reds, and he powders one over the right-field fence, on a line against a building across the street from the park. It was then I changed my mind about the chances of a pitcher becoming the first person killed by a batted ball. I decided that the first victim would be some guy walking along Western Avenue, minding his own business, who would be conked by one of Kluszewski's home runs." ◆

The 1953 All-Star Game

The second and last All-Star Game held at Crosley Field was staged on July 14, 1953, and featured the only All-Star Game appearance by the legendary Satchel Paige. A crowd of 30,846 watched the National League defeat the American League, 5-1.

Paige, representing the St. Louis Browns, relieved in the eighth inning with the National League leading, 3-0. According to the *Enquirer*, the 47-year-old "Satchemo" gave the spectators the most entertaining moments of the afternoon with his "weird motions on the mound and his obvious aversion to doing something in one minute, which could be stretched to five…."

Before the game Paige promised to throw his famous "nothing ball." "It ain't got nothing on it, but they don't hit it," he explained. However, his old colleague from the Negro Leagues, Dodger catcher Roy Campanella, hit one of the change-ups for a single, and hits by Enos Slaughter and Pirates pitcher Murray Dickson scored the Nationals' fourth and fifth runs.

Most baseball experts predicted a high-scoring contest in cozy Crosley Field, led by the powerful slugging of Ted Kluszewski, Gus Bell, Stan Musial, Duke Snider, Eddie Mathews, Yogi Berra, and Micky Mantle. (Eighteen future Hall of Famers appeared in the game.) But a brisk wind blowing in from left field, and the strong pitching of Robin Roberts, Warren Spahn, Curt Simmons, and Billy Pierce kept the ball in the park, and resulted in just one extra base hit, a double by Pee Wee Reese.

The Cardinals Enos Slaughter was the star of the game with two hits, two runs scored, a stolen base, and a sliding catch of Harvey Kuenn's line drive.

Hundreds of shirt-sleeved fans crowded the Crosley Field ticket windows along Findlay Street the morning of the 1953 All-Star Game. Nearby, scalpers sold $5 tickets for $15.

Mickey Mantle was the favorite of the autograph-hungry youngsters, but the biggest attraction for the press was a player not even in uniform. Boston Red Sox outfielder Ted Williams had just been discharged from the Marines after his tour of duty in the Korean War, and this was his first public appearance.

Photographers and writers surrounded Williams in the American League dugout. When National League president Warren Giles spotted Williams he said, "I'm glad you're here and I'm glad you're not playing!" Moments later, Williams threw out the first ball to the roar of the crowd. ◆

Gus Bell (left) and Ted Kluszewski (right) started the 1953 All-Star Game as representatives of the Cincinnati Redlegs.
Klu was the number one vote-getter in the fan balloting, establishing himself as the most popular player in baseball. The two disappointed the home crowd by managing just one hit in seven at bats, a

Kluszewski single. But the Cincinnati fans still gave NL manager Chuck Dressen (center) the raspberries when he lifted the Redlegs for pinch hitters. "Chuck took his own life into his hands in Cincinnati when he dared to take out Kluszewski and Bell," laughed NL All-Star Jackie Robinson.

Crosley's Best: Frank Robinson

So fondly did Frank Robinson regard Crosley Field, that when the Baltimore Orioles were building a new green cathedral – Oriole Park at Camden Yards – Robinson tried to talk the club into building a grassy rise from the edge of the outfield to the outfield wall.

"Just like the terrace at Crosley Field," said the smiling former Reds great who also starred with the Orioles. "But they wouldn't go for it."

That was two decades after the last game was played at Crosley Field.

Robinson played for the Reds from 1956 through 1965.

Over those ten seasons, he averaged .303, 32 home runs, 32 doubles, 5 triples, 101 RBI, 104 runs scored and 16 stolen bases in 150 games. Nobody at Findlay and Western ever combined power, speed, batting average and fearlessness at the plate and on the basepaths the way number 20 did.

"No one was more mentally tough than him," said former Dodgers pitcher Stan Williams. "If you knocked him on his ass three times in a row and came anywhere near the plate the fourth time, he'd hit it a country mile. You didn't want to wake him up. But it was hard not to because he stood right on the plate and leaned over, so you had no choice but to pitch him in. There was always a good chance you'd knock him down. Then he became more dangerous."

And nowhere was he more dangerous than Crosley Field.

"Of all the places I played in either league, Crosley Field was my favorite ballpark," said Robinson. "It was a unique, quaint ballpark. We were close to the fans. We came out to the field and went back into the clubhouse right between the fans. You got to know the fans and they got to know you on a personal-type basis."

Was there anything Robinson didn't like about Crosley Field?

"Yes, the scoreboard with the big clock in left-center field – that thing was about 55 feet high! Do you realize how many home runs that took away? Then again, how many ballparks don't have a 400-foot mark? It was 380 to center field.... So, Crosley Field took something away, but it gave something up, too."

On April 17, 1956, 21-year-old rookie Frank Robinson made his major-league debut.

"I still remember that day like it was yesterday," wrote Robinson in his autobiography, *My Life Is Baseball*. "It was a raw, cloudy afternoon with the temperature in the forties. There was an overflow crowd at Crosley Field, some of the spectators spilling over into the outfield. That meant that any ball hit into the crowd would be a ground-rule double, and I remember asking myself what I was going to do if I had to go back for a long fly?

"The game was scoreless going into the last of the second inning. Then Ray Jablonski came up and hit a home run. The crowd was still buzzing about Jabbo's home run when I dug in the batter's box, awaiting the first pitch of my major-league career. Going unnoticed like that was fine by me, it made me feel nice and relaxed. I don't think Vinegar Bend Mizell was too concerned about me, a rookie, in his first at-bat. He gave me the fastball right

Frank Robinson checked into the Reds spring training camp in Tampa, Florida in 1959. Robinson may have had some extra gloves in his bag. He had played left field his first three seasons, but was switched to first base for the '59 season. He returned to the outfield in 1961.

During the '59 spring training camp, Robinson and the Reds made their annual visit to Havanna to play exhibition games, but it was the last trip to Cuba the club would make due to the Castro revolution.

Crosley Field

down the middle. I hit it off the center field wall for a double, missing a home run by a couple of feet."

"That '56 team was a fun team," recalled Robinson. "Nobody treated me like a rookie. I was accepted by the players and that helped me right away. They made me feel at home from day one. The manager, Birdie Tebbetts, didn't put any pressure on me. He told the writers, 'If he hits .260 with 15 home runs and 60 RBI, I'll be satisfied.' I knew I could do better than than, and Birdie knew it, too."

Robinson hit .290, with 38 home runs and 83 RBI. He led the league in runs scored with 122 and was named National League Rookie of the Year. He was hit by pitches 20 times – by far the NL leader. Robinson had not even adopted his menacing crowd-the-plate batting style until spring training of 1956.

"In the minors I stood deep in the box and away from the plate, and that worked well enough against minor-league pitching," he wrote in *My Life Is Baseball*. "(But in the majors) I would be up against pitchers who were much smarter than me, who had been around a long time, who had much more experience and better control, especially on their breaking pitches. I asked myself, 'What am I going to do to neutralize the experience the pitchers have over me?'

"I decided to move up on the plate. Pitchers like to have the whole plate to work with – to come in on you and then go away from you. I decided I wouldn't give them the complete plate to shoot at....I stood about even with home plate with my feet up against the chalk line in front of the batter's box, bent slightly from the waist, hanging my head in what they call 'concussion

On Opening Day, 1963, Frank Robinson blasted a two-run home run against the Pirates on the way to a Reds victory, 5-2. On deck was Gordy Coleman; kneeling next to Coleman was batboy and future equipment manager, Bernie Stowe.

Despite hitting 21 homers, driving in 92 runs, and stealing 26 bases, the Reds thought Robby had an off-year in 1963 since he only hit .259. He took a $5,000 cut in his 1964 contract ($55,000 down from $60,000), but said he deserved it. "...after the season I had last year, I knew I had to take a cut. All things considered, I have been treated fairly."

alley,' so I could get a good look at the pitch….Right away that spring, I began to hit the ball good."

A more difficult proposition for rookie Robinson in 1956 was left field.

"Playing the terrace was difficult for me that first season," he said. "It was steepest in left field, not quite as bad in center and right. I'd never known another ballpark with a terrace, except the old ballpark in Nashville. Every time a ball was hit over your head at Crosley Field, it was a new experience. You couldn't run up the terrace; you almost had to climb it. And when you got to the top of it, there was the brick wall. When you got up there and the ball was over your head, it would come off that wall like a missile.

"I came to enjoy the challenge of playing out there. It was very, very tough on visiting outfielders. I remember Willie Mays winding up flat on his back. You couldn't prepare yourself to play that outfield. You had to do it."

In 1958, 22-year-old Vada Pinson joined Robinson on the Reds. They'd gone to the same high school in Oakland, but didn't know each other well. They were three years apart. They quickly became inseparable – on the field, in the clubhouse and away from the park. In 1959, Pinson's first full season, Robinson drove in 125 runs, his first 100-plus RBI season. Pinson scored 131 runs to lead the National League. So impressed was the Reds management after Pinson's rookie season (.316 batting average, 47 doubles, 20 home runs and 21 stolen bases) that then-Reds general manager Gabe Paul said, "I don't say I wouldn't trade him, but (Reds owner) Powel Crosley told me to be sure to include myself in any deal."

Pinson was one of the fastest players in the game – his speed to first base was a scintillating 3.3 seconds. In seven of his 10 full seasons with the Reds, he stole 20 or more bases. He led the league twice in hits, doubles, and triples. For five straight seasons (1959-63), he never missed a game.

Pinson hit for average and power, too, hitting 20 or more home runs six times in his Cincinnati career. Robinson though was always the big bopper. In his book, *The Long Season*, Jim Brosnan recalled that Pinson, after hitting a home run, ran around the bases like he was trying to beat out a bunt. "Robby shakes Vada's hand when he gets to the bench and says, 'Little man, you just better stick to singles and leave the long ones to us cats who know how to act 'em out.'"

In 1961, Pinson batted .343 and helped the Reds win the pennant. Robinson hit .323 with 37 home runs and 124 RBI and scored 117 runs. He was named NL Most Valuable Player.

Living a block away from Crosley Field on Poplar Street during all this was a young boy named Dave Parker. He used to stand in the players' parking lot and watch in awe as Robinson and Pinson pulled up in identical white Thunderbirds with porthole windows and red interiors. One day Robinson popped open the trunk and handed Parker an extra outfielder's glove.

"That clinched him as my idol," said Parker, a future Reds slugger, who as a teenager took a job at Crosley selling lemonade on sultry days and hot dogs at night games, but was more interested in watching his idol play than he was in making pocket change.

Robinson and Pinson, together in the Reds lineup for seven seasons, inspired countless kids with their power, speed, and grace. Toughness, too, was a trait that became a Robinson trademark. In the first game of a doubleheader with the Braves at Crosley Field in 1960, Robinson was tagged out at third by Eddie Mathews. Robby had come in with spikes flying and the two were soon exchanging punches. Robinson definitely was the loser, with a swollen right eye and a sprained thumb, and he had to retire to the locker room.

But he never gave a thought to sitting out the second game. Robby had a home run and a double in the Reds 4-0 win, and robbed Mathews of a hit on a diving catch in left field.

Of such heroics are legends made. Unfortunately for Reds fans, the heroics ended prematurely in 1965, when general manager Bill Dewitt traded Robinson to the Orioles. Robinson was "an old 30," said DeWitt. The "old man" promptly won the M.V.P. award in the American League and eventually made the Hall of Fame.

Over the years, the Reds have officially retired only two numbers: 1 for Fred Hutchinson, and 5 for Johnny Bench.

But for all those fans who saw him play at Crosley Field, number 20 will always belong to Frank Robinson.   ◆

A muscular Vada Pinson (left) compared bats with Frank Robinson. Although Pinson is not remembered as power hitter, the 5'11", 170 pound center fielder hit 20 home runs or more seven times. Pinson was also durable; he once played 508 consecutive games. Pinson and Robinson played together with the Reds from 1958 through 1965.

Pinson went on to play 11 seasons with the Reds; he was traded to St. Louis in 1969.

Pinson played more games than any other player at Crosley Field, some 780 games. Robinson was second, followed by Edd Roush, Roy McMillan, and Ted Kluszewski.

The Slugging Redlegs

The 1950s was a home run era for the National League, and there was no better place to watch the long ball hitters than Crosley Field. In 1954, 1956, 1957, and 1959, more home runs were hit in Crosley Field than any other National League park.

Crosley, which had never had a reputation as a home run park because of its deep fences, became a hitters' playground in the 1953 season when the club installed additional seats in front of the right field bleachers, reducing the right field foul line distance from 366 feet to 342 feet (see page 146). The Redlegs responded. The club had hit 104 home runs at Crosley in 1952, but in 1953, they smashed 166, led by left-handed sluggers Ted Kluszewski,

Gus Bell, and Willard Marshall.

This right field seating area, which became known as the "Goat Run," remained in place through the 1958 season, and in those six years, the Redlegs averaged 171 home runs a year, 100 of them hit at home. But the year that will forever live in Reds history was 1956, when the Redlegs almost won the pennant on home run power alone, hitting 221 homers which tied the Major League mark first set by the Giants in 1947, and later surpassed by the New York Yankees in 1961. (The 221 mark is still the National League record.)

The 1956 club surprised fans by challenging for the pennant until the final week of the season, and drawing one million for the first time, but the Redlegs finished third to the Dodgers and Braves. With the pennant hopes over, the only question was whether the club could set a new home run record. In the next-to-last game of the year in Chicago, back-up catcher and pinch hitter Smokey Burgess tied the record in the eighth inning with his 12th home run. But a "strong wind blowing in off Lake Michigan," as described by the *Enquirer's* Lou Smith, kept even the Reds from hitting a home run out of Wrigley Field in the final game. ◆

Rookie Frank Robinson (left) and veteran Ted Kluszewski (right) combined for 73 home runs in 1956, making manager Birdie Tebbetts a happy man. Robinson's 38 homers tied the major league mark for home runs by a rookie.

Reds Bomb Western Avenue

In a four-game weekend series with the Milwaukee Braves in July, 1954, the Reds hit seven home runs. Two were by left fielder Jim Greengrass, who hit 27 homers and drove in 95 runs in 1954. Chuck Harmon, Cincinnati's first black player, hit one off the laundry in left field. Three of the home runs, by Bell, Post, and Greengrass, fell into the "Goat Run" section at the base of the right field bleachers. Greengrass's home run to left center was the longest, clearing the scoreboard clock and landing in the middle of the intersection.

Crosley Field

Jack Siebler, of Siebler Tailors , presented 11 suits to Reds outfielder Wally Post in the 12 seasons Post played with the Reds, one for each time Post hit the Siebler suit sign atop the laundry beyond the left field wall. Siebler's sign was erected in the late 1930s, and came down after the 1960 season when the laundry was razed for parking.

Ernie Lombardi was the suit leader until Post took the crown. Willie Mays led the visitors.

On Opening Day, 1955, Ted Kluszewski was crowned the king of "crunch," and was presented with a commemorative bat by the Findlay Market Association for leading the major leagues in home runs. Klu hit 49 home runs and drove in 141 RBI in 1954.

Inspecting the scepter were, left to right, Wally Post, Jim Greengrass, Kluszewski, Gus Bell, and Ray Jablonski. Jablonski had just joined the Reds and started at third base in 1955 and 1956.

Of the above sluggers, only Jim Greengrass was not a member of the fabled 1956 club. In that record-setting year, Post hit 36, Kluszewski, 35, Bell, 29, and Jablonski, 15.

Other home run hitters in 1956 were Frank Robinson, 38, Ed Bailey, 28, Smokey Burgess, 12, George Crowe, 10, Bob Thurman, 8, Roy McMillan, 3, Johnny Temple, 2, Stan Palys, 2, Joe Frazier, 1, and Joe Nuxhall chipped in for the pitching staff with 2.

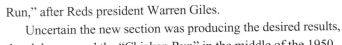

A New Scoreboard and the "Goat Run"

The most significant changes made in the ballpark in the 1950s involved the on-again, off-again temporary seating section in right field, and the erection of a new scoreboard in 1957. The club also added murals and Reds Hall of Fame plaques beneath the grandstand in the concession areas to honor players.

The right field seating section was first installed in 1946, when the Reds wanted to increase both seating and home runs. This reduced the left field line from 366 feet (the longest in the major leagues) to 342 feet and shortened the distance to right center from 387 feet to 375 feet. This section, which eventually came to be known as the "Goat Run," was first called "Giles Chicken Run," after Reds president Warren Giles.

Uncertain the new section was producing the desired results, the club removed the "Chicken Run" in the middle of the 1950 season. But the result of that move was felt immediately. Crosley went from the fifth best home run park in the National League to the worst. Prior to the 1953 season, the section was rebuilt. It acquired the new nickname of the "Goat Run," and it remained up through the 1958 season.

Perhaps the most familiar landmark of the late-Crosley era was the five-story scoreboard erected in 1957. It replaced Matty Schwab's original scoreboard which was built in 1912 and extensively remodeled in 1934. The new board was 58 feet high, including the clock, and 65 feet wide.

Inside, five scorers scurried over three floors of scaffolding and planks, keeping the numbers up-to-date. Some of the information, such as balls, strikes, outs, hits, runs, and errors was flashed electronically. The lineups and the out-of-town games were changed manually.

In 1957, two UC students and three Western Hills High School seniors ran the operation. Their biggest surprise of the summer came when Wally Post crushed a ball through the home half of the second inning glass. "It stunned us at first with glass flying all over the place," one said, "but we got a ball." ◆

The "Goat Run" reduced the right field line to 342 feet, which was still the second-longest right field line in the National League. By the mid-1950s, when this picture was taken, the bleachers had been christened the "Sun Deck."

Workers installed the team name plates on the new scoreboard just one week before Opening Day, 1957. The massive 58-foot tall structure was in play, and it snared many a ball that would have gone for a home run over the old scoreboard. The original advertising signs included Gem Razor, Marlboro, Hudepohl, and Ford.

The scoreboard operators peered out openings to follow the game. A ticker tape machine kept them up-to-date on out-of-town scores. If the wrong information was posted anywhere on the board, public address announcer Paul Sommerkamp would alert the chief operator via a special phone line.

Crosley Field

King Car Changes a Neighborhood

The pennant-contending, home-run bashing Redlegs of 1956 brought a season of unforgettable memories to the fans of Crosley Field, but as it turned out, the season also spelled the doom of baseball at Findlay and Western.

The incompatibility of the automobile and the narrow streets of the neighborhood around Crosley had been noted as far back as 1925 when club president Garry Herrmann unsuccessfully lobbied for moving the Reds out of the crowded West End. And, this proposal came when public transportation was still the most popular means of travel within the city. But the rise of the automobile and the decline of public transportation after the war, combined with the one million-plus fans of 1956, placed such a stress on the neighborhood's transportation system that a decision about Crosley's future could no longer be postponed.

Crosley Field was landlocked: dense residential and manufacturing areas on three sides, and railroad yards to the west. There was not enough street parking nor enough parking lots. In the mid-50s, there was only one large lot near the ballpark, one block south on Dalton, which held 400 cars (at 50 cents a car). Residents met the increasing demand by parking cars in their driveways and yards. And some young kids tried to cash in by offering fans "protection" for their cars parked on the streets, in effect charging them not to vandalize their autos.

Increasingly, city leaders spoke of a new baseball park – although no one knew exactly when or where – but in the short-term, owner Powel Crosley wanted the city to provide 5,000 additional parking spaces near his ballpark. The city finally approved a $2 million dollar plan in 1958, but negotiating with property

This parking lot north of Dalton Street, just south of Crosley Field, was filled in 1961 for a twi-night double header with St. Louis. Despite this and other new lots, the traffic jam for this game extended across the Ohio River into Northern Kentucky.

148

Crosley Field

owners further delayed the opening of the first lots until the 1959 season.

Additional money for off-street parking became available when construction of I-75, or the Millcreek Expressway as it was then called, was approved. The route ran adjacent to Western Avenue, and the city began clearing land in 1960 for temporary parking areas.

However, during the three-year standstill from 1956 to 1959, owner Crosley chaffed at the delays, and for the first time the city heard rumors the Reds might leave. In 1957, the Cincinnati press quoted New York sources saying the Reds could move to New York to replace the Dodgers and Giants who were heading west. The Reds denied the story, but Crosley later warned that he could not understand the delay when other cities wanted Cincinnati's franchise.

"There are so many other cities ready to offer a stadium, adequate parking space and everything of that sort, practically for nothing....(I)n this competitive situation...we are entitled to ask for...some additional parking space."

The land was eventually cleared, but at a tremendous loss to the West End. All the familiar Crosley landmarks also disappeared, including the left field laundry and Hase Cafe, a Findlay Street institution since 1914. ◆

Prior to a night game in 1961, cars inched along Dalton Street heading north towards Crosley Field.

Crosley Field

The photographs on this and the next page were taken six years apart, and document the massive changes in the neighborhood surrounding Crosley Field created by the construction of I-75 and parking lots for the ballpark. The above picture, looking south, was taken in 1956, when the Reds' attendance topped one million for the first time. The most prominent parking lot lay south of Crosley, on the west side of Dalton Street. Cincinnati's major railroad station, Union Terminal, is at the top of the photograph, some eight blocks south of Crosley Field. Many fans on special excursion trains walked to and from the ballpark from Union Terminal.

This photograph was taken looking southeast on Opening Day, 1962. The I-75 expressway path had been cleared adjacent to Western Avenue and most buildings within several blocks of Crosley Field had been demolished. The outfield landmarks, including the laundry behind the left field wall, were gone.

Crosley Field was no longer a neighborhood park. It had become an island amidst a sea of parking lots and highways, a look that anticipated the modern ballparks, including Riverfront Stadium, that were designed to accommodate the automobile.

Crosley Field

A New Crosley?

The question of a new baseball stadium for Cincinnati burst onto the local scene in the mid-1950s and dominated downtown development discussions for the next decade. The real or imagined threat of the Reds leaving Cincinnati turned idle speculation about ballpark improvements into serious planning for a new stadium.

At first, nothing about a new ballpark was settled:

- Could Crosley Field be renovated?
- Should Crosley be demolished and a new park built on its site?
- Should a new park be built in another location?
- Where should a new park be located? Downtown? Suburbs?

Since 1948, the city's long-term planning guide had called for a new stadium to be located downtown near the Ohio River. But the Cincinnati riverfront in the mid-1950s was an eyesore of industrial sites, dilapidated buildings, and junkyards. To the Reds, and to many baseball fans, the location offered no improvement over the deteriorating neighborhood surrounding Crosley Field. Suburban sites drew far more interest from the public, as did the idea of improving Crosley Field. Proposed sites included:

- the northern suburb of Blue Ash;
- Lunken Airport in the near-eastern suburbs;
- Hamilton County Fairgrounds, eight miles north of Crosley;
- the vast mall area in front of Union Terminal.

Proposed improvements to Crosley Field included creating additional parking lots, building a 4,000 seat grandstand beyond the left field wall, and adding 35 private, plexiglass-enclosed boxes in the rear of the lower deck. One plan that surfaced in 1965 called for a new domed stadium on the Crosley site. (That idea

was vetoed by the West End Community Council who opposed further demolition of their neighborhood and displacement of families.)

One of the first designs for a new Cincinnati ballpark appeared on the front page of *The Cincinnati Post* on June 6, 1957 (see below). "A Dream of a Stadium," headlined the paper. Although

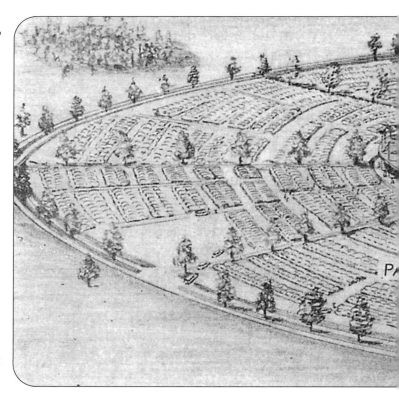

these plans were not incorporated in the final design of Riverfront Stadium, they provide insight into what people envisioned a "dream" of a baseball stadium would include in the mid-'50s

Appearing like something out of the Jetsons, with swooping light towers and an elliptical roof, the proposed stadium included 45,000 seats, three heliports, a train siding, and parking for 20,000 cars. The architects, the Cincinnati firm of Vogt, Ivers, Seaman, and Associates, did not identify a specific site, but assumed it would be located near a rail line and one of the city's new expressways. They estimated the cost at $8 million.

Anticipating a trend that would characterize most new parks built in the 1960s and 1970s, the architects created uniform outfield dimensions, so uniform in fact that all distances from home plate measured an identical 375 feet. The architects also considered the idea of enclosing the entire stadium in plexiglass, but predicted that the cost of a cooling system would prove prohibitive. A transparent dome covering was assumed because

light would be required to grow grass. Of course, this was prior to the discovery of Astroturf.

Such plans served to stimulate discussion about a new stadium, but were premature. Unlike the last time Cincinnati built a baseball park, in 1912, the approval and construction of a new stadium at mid-century would involve more than just the club owners, and would take more than a year.

Unhappy with the delays, but finally convinced of the city's desire to solve the Reds' stadium problem, Powel Crosley signed an agreement in 1958 to keep the team in Cincinnati through 1963. This gave planners a reprieve and by the mid-1960s, the city was clearly committed to building a new stadium. The Reds would remain in Cincinnati, but Crosley Field's days were numbered. ◆

These 1957 plans for a new Cincinnati ballpark included three levels of seating. The cantilever style of construction eliminated all posts, a frequent criticism of the Crosley Field grandstand.

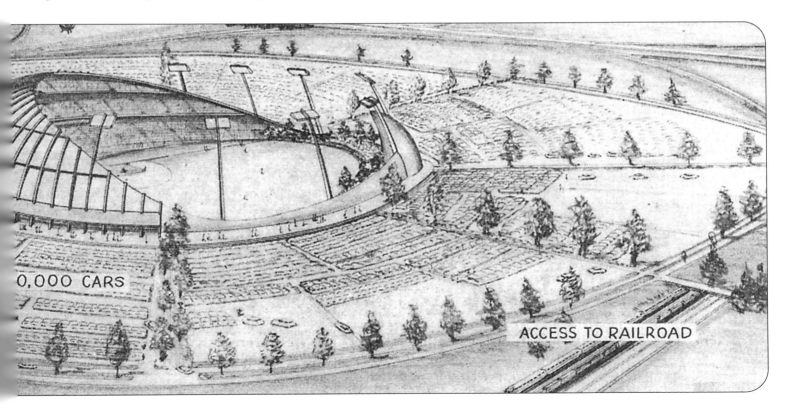

0,000 CARS

ACCESS TO RAILROAD

Promotions!

Promotions and special events had a long history at Findlay and Western, dating all the way back to the pre-Crosley era when president Aaron Stern offered free admission to "ladies" when the Reds handsome pitcher, Tony Mullane, pitched in 1886. In the 1930s, general manager Larry McPhail brought in college bands and staged a fireworks show before each night game.

By the 1950s, there was a regular lineup of annual promotions

that often drew big crowds. Although promotions continued into the Riverfront Stadium era, the cozy atmosphere of Crosley, and the policy of allowing fans on the field for the pre-game activities, gave the Crosley Field promotions a unique feel.

Joe Nuxhall recalled the fan appreciation nights from the 1950s. "Before the game all of us Reds players would go up in the stands. We'd start shaking hands with the fans. When the whistle blew, whoever's hand we were shaking would go down on the field with us, and we'd introduce them over the PA system. They'd get some type of gift, a radio, something nice. It was fun, a great time. You couldn't help but be close with fans at Crosley."

One of the biggest annual events, second only to Opening Day, was Shrine Night, when the elaborately-costumed Shriners paraded on the field. Several nearby cities had their own special days, popular players were feted with gifts, even new cars, and there was Farmer's Night, complete with a milking contest.

Pitcher Jim Brosnan, in his book, *The Long Season*, recalled Family Night at Crosley, when the players and families were honored. Brosnan speculated that the fans saved their loudest cheers for the biggest families: "Gus Bell, a hunk of potent virility the likes of which has seldom been seen in organized baseball, had seven Bells ring around him. The applause was deafening." ◆

Left: On Camera Day, fans could pose with the Reds players, such as catcher Johnny Edwards.

Right: A fleet of buses hauled fans to Crosley from Hamilton, Ohio for the annual Hamilton Night promotion. Youth baseball teams marched around the field, and Hamilton native Joe Nuxhall was always honored.

On July 23, 1957, the Reds held a fan appreciation night and passed out gifts to winning ticket holders.

Reds players, from left to right, were Roy McMillan, Frank Robinson, Brooks Lawrence, and Don Hoak.

Joe Nuxhall remembered the night in 1958 when bandleader Vaughn Monroe played at Crosley before a game, and his act featured a singer named Dagmar.

"I'll never forget when the guys set me up when Dagmar came in. She was a blonde bombshell, a Jayne Mansfield type. Dagmar asked for somebody to go up on stage and dance with her. I wasn't going to do it, but I think it was Klu who set me up. I remembered I stepped on Dagmar's foot by accident. I had my spikes on. That ended the dance right there."

On July 5, 1960, the Gus Bell family posed on Reds Family Night at Crosley Field. The Bell entourage included, from left, Joyce Bell, Terry, 3, Gus Bell, Debbie, 9, Becky, 4, Timmie, 6, Buddy, 8, and Randy, 7.

Buddy Bell eventually followed his father into professional baseball, and played for the Reds from 1985 to 1988.

In 1959, the Reds honored the 1939-40 National League and World Champion teams. Among the players attending the event were Ernie Lombardi, manager Bill McKechnie, Johnny Vander Meer, Paul Derringer, and Frank McCormick.

In 1958, the club inaugurated the Reds Hall of Fame, and held induction ceremonies each year. The Hall of Fame plaques hung in the concession areas under the Crosley Field grandstand.

Crosley Field

1960-1969: Shadows Fall

A young Pete Rose gave some batting tips to a fan at Crosley Field. Rose, Rookie of the Year in 1963, quickly became the most popular Red of the 1960s.

CROSLEY'S LAST DECADE BEGAN AMIDST THE CLATTER OF WRECKING balls and earth-moving equipment as the area around the ballpark was cleared for new parking lots and the construction of I-75. Despite the parking improvements and talk of modernizing the park, it became obvious by the mid-1960s that Crosley Field could not survive. The deterioration of the neighborhood, the continuing frustration with parking, Crosley's size and age, and the new stadium boom in other cities, plus increasing public sentiment for a new park, spelled Crosley's doom. The Reds, the new NFL Bengals, and the city finally agreed on a multi-use stadium on the river.

While controversy about the future of Crosley swirled outside the park, the Reds shrugged it all aside and had the best decade in their history. Inside the park, the club created plenty of excitement with a surprise pennant-winner in 1961, brash rookie stars in 1963 and 1968, near pennant-winning seasons in 1964, 1965, and 1969, and a decade-long winning percentage of .537 that was the best to that point in Reds history.

Nearly nine million fans attended games, including two seasons over one million. Several new parking lots around Crosley added 2,500 spaces, and in a 1961 press release, the club estimated that there were now over 6,000 parking spaces in the municipal and private lots near the park. That did not include the temporary "parking lot" and the free view from the I-75 construction zone behind the center field wall. Unlike the renegade bleacherites of decades past who had used factory windows and roofs for a free outfield seat, the 1960 "roadies" sat in the back of pick-up trucks and on car roofs.

Ticket prices at Crosley changed little in the 1960s. In 1961, box seats were $3, reserved grandstand seats, $2.25, and unreserved grandstand $1.50. The Sun Deck was 75 cents. In 1969, prices were $3.50 for box seats, $2.50 for reserved grandstand, and $1.50 for general admission, including the Sun Deck. ◆

Jim Maloney was on the mound for the 1967 opener, and was the winning pitcher in a 6-1 win over the Dodgers.

While the interior of the park changed little in the 1960s, the appearance of the park changed dramatically with the demolition of the landmark buildings beyond the outfield fences in 1960-61.

Opening Days in the '60s also had a different look with the club abandoning the tradition of seating the overflow crowd in the outfield. Contrast this photograph of Opening Day, 1967, with the photograph on pages 128-29.

The new glass backstop (replacing the screen wire), and an extension of the center field wall are visible in this photo. The wall was raised nine and one-half feet in 1963 to a height of 23 feet to block the view of construction on I-75. The plywood extension consisted of two rows of ping-pong tables, supported by cross beams.

When first built, the extension was not in play. Any ball hit above the concrete wall was a home run. Umpires listened for the sound of the ball striking the fence to help make a close call. In 1969, after several disputed calls, the entire fence was put in play; a home run had to clear the wall.

Prior to the 1961 season, the Superior Laundry and other businesses lined the north side of York Street, just beyond the left field wall. Kids climbed the telephone poles for a long distance view of the action, and hoped for a home run ball to clear the fence.

This photograph was taken during the 1940s, and included the rear of the old scoreboard.

Although York Street was barely more than an alley, it played a prominent role in the history of Crosley Field. In 1921, the first major league home run ever hit over the fence, off the bat of Reds left fielder, Pat Duncan, landed there.

In 1919, the club built temporary bleachers over York Street for the World Series. In the early 1960s, the club considered building permanent stands in this location, but the city would not permit the closing of York.

After the 1960 season, the city cleared out the area north of Crosley Field for additional parking. The laundry, the most famous landmark in the history of Crosley Field, and one of the best known in all of baseball, was demolished for 38 parking spaces.

This photograph, taken in the early 1960s, included the rear of the new scoreboard erected in 1957 and the 40-foot-high netting over the left field wall. The netting, which was not in play, was erected in 1961 to protect cars in the parking lots.

Crosley Field

A Changing of the the Guard

On the eve of the 1961 season, on March 28, Powel Crosley, Jr. died of a heart attack. The 74-year-old Crosley, who had owned the Reds for 27 years and given the ballpark his name, passed along controlling interest in the club in his will to his only daughter, Mrs. Stanley Kess.

In his last years, Crosley had divested himself of his other business interests, including appliances, broadcasting, and the Crosley car, but he had retained ownership of the Reds. Crosley's clubs had played in two World Series, and if he had survived another year, he would have seen his Reds in a third fall classic.

Not that Crosley would have expected a pennant winner at Crosley Field in 1961. The Reds had finished 20 games out of

From his private box on top of the grandstand, Powel Crosley watched the crowd gather for the opening of the 1959 season.

first place with a 67-87 record in 1960, and no club in the history of baseball had ever won a pennant after a .435 season. When general manager Gabe Paul left after the 1959 season, Crosley hired William O. DeWitt. After sizing up his team for a year, DeWitt and manager Fred Hutchinson mapped out a strategy for 1961 that resulted in a complete shakeup of the team.

DeWitt, who also assumed most of the executive duties of the club when Crosley died, traded for Joey Jay, Gene Freese, and Don Blasingame, brought up Gordy Coleman and Johnny Edwards from the minors, and dumped Roy McMillan, Cal McClish, Billy Martin, and Ed Bailey. Hutchinson shuffled his lineup, moving Frank Robinson to right field and Eddie Kasko to shortstop and he platooned Gus Bell and Wall Post in left field.

Every general manager dreams of making all the right moves. As it turned out, DeWitt did. According to baseball historian Bill James, in the pre-free agency era, Bill DeWitt and the Reds were the only organization ever to "take a bad team, make a series of trades, and immediately come out of it with a championship team."

In the pre-season polls, not one of 232 sportswriters picked Cincinnati first in the National League. But the Reds won the pennant and DeWitt looked like a genius. Five years later, though, the fans were calling for his head after the dismal Frank Robinson-for-Milt Pappas trade, rated as one of the worst in Reds history.

Off the field, DeWitt continued the complex negotiations Crosley had begun with the city over the future of Crosley Field and a new stadium. DeWitt opposed the eventual deal of a shared stadium with the Bengals and he sold the club in 1966 (he had bought it from Kess). Francis Dale, publisher of the *Enquirer,* became president of the Reds, and Robert Howsam became the general manager, the leadership team that would take the Reds into the Riverfront Stadium era. ◆

Bill DeWitt, the general manager and later president of the Reds, displayed a commemorative photo mural of Powel Crosley to Crosley's daughter, Mrs. Stanley Kess, and manager Fred Hutchinson. The mural depicted highlights from Powel Crosley's life, and hung under the grandstand in the concession area behind home plate. Kess became the principal stockholder of the Reds upon Crosley's death, and later sold her interests to DeWitt.

The Miracle on Western Avenue

Maybe it was the club's new policy of beer in the clubhouse. Maybe it was the fire of manager Fred Hutchinson. Maybe it was Frank Robinson's MVP year. Or, maybe, as relief pitcher Jim Brosnan said in his book, *Pennant Race*, it was because "on this club…either you did or somebody did it for you."

The 1961 "Ragamuffin Reds," the team nobody picked to win the pennant, picked each other up all year long, fought off losing slumps, won the big games when they had to, and finally captured the NL pennant by four games over the favored Dodgers.

The season began with a whimper. The club looked miserable in spring training, and lost eight in a row on an April West Coast trip. But they immediately turned around and won nine in a row.

Coach Reggie Otero complained, "One day we play so lousy, I can't sleep at night, then next day we play like champions."

In June, the Reds moved into first place for the first time. But by August they had dropped to second, and they met the Dodgers in LA down two games to them in the standings. Now, the favored Dodgers would finally put these upstarts away and return some sanity to the National League, so thought the sporting press. But instead, the Reds swept LA, moved into first, and never relinquished the lead.

The final showdown of the year came in late August at Crosley Field, when the Dodgers visited Cincinnati for a four-game series. The fans filled Crosley with their red and white "Root the Reds Home" pennants, and watched Hutch's crew win a Sunday doubleheader that ended the Dodgers' hopes.

On September 26, the Reds beat the Cubs at Wrigley Field and when the Dodgers lost, the pennant belonged to the Reds for the first time in 21 years. A wild, spontaneous celebration at Fountain Square lasted long into the night.

In the closing days of the season, Jim Brosnan jokingly worried that "we'll win the pennant and Khrushchev will drop a bomb on New York and ruin the series."

His teammate Sherman "Roadblock" Jones astutely noted, "We wouldn't have to play the Yankees then, would we?"

There were no bombs, and the Reds met the Yankees, led by the "M & M" boys, Roger Maris and Mickey Mantle, in the series. Giving the Reds no respect, the New York writers wondered if the Yankees would win in three games. The Yanks won the opener, but to everyone's surprise, the Reds captured the second game and headed back to Crosley tied 1-1. After the game, Hutch needled the New York writers: "Do you think it'll go three?"

The Cincinnati faithful had already grabbed up tickets for the three games at Crosley. In fact the club had to stop accepting requests after receiving 146,000 orders for the approximately 45,000 reserved grandstand seats available (at $8.20 a ticket). No box seats were available for public sale, having been allotted to season ticket holders. The club placed unreserved bleacher seats ($4.10) and standing room ($2.05) on sale on October 4 at its downtown Vine Street office and at the ballpark, where thousands stood in line.

Hutch hoped the familiar confines of Crosley Field would help the Reds. "It takes a pitcher longer to learn this park," he said. Yogi Berra, the Yankees left fielder worried about the terrace. "It's as bad coming down it as it is going up."

The third game, on Saturday, October 7, proved to be the best of the series, and for the 32,589 Crosley fans, the most heartbreaking. The Reds led 2-1 in the eighth inning when pinch-hitter John Blanchard homered. Then in the ninth, Maris smacked a Bob Purkey pitch into the bleachers and the Yankees won, 3-2.

The dramatic home run seemed to sap the Reds' spirit. They lost the next two games, 7-0 and 13-5, and the series, four games to one. The Reds, who hit .270 during the season, were a weak .206 in the series. Hutch sat in his office after game five, and faced the obvious. "I have to say the better team won," he admitted. ◆

Prior to the 1961 season, Frank Robinson was convicted on a concealed weapons charge. The press played up the incident and the fans criticized him, but once the season began Robby quickly put the episode to rest. He hit .323, with 37 home runs and 117 RBI and was named MVP. He slumped to .200 in the series with one homer.

Crosley Field

Pitcher Bob Purkey was swamped for autographs at Crosley Field in the summer of 1961. Although the Reds of this era are remembered more for their hitting than pitching, the 1961 club finished second in the National League in team ERA.

Jim O'Toole (19-9), Joey Jay (21-10), and Purkey (16-12) were the big three of the staff. Right-hander Jim Brosnan and lefty Bill Henry gave Hutchinson a powerful combination out of the bullpen. The two saved 32 games and the club led the league in saves with 40.

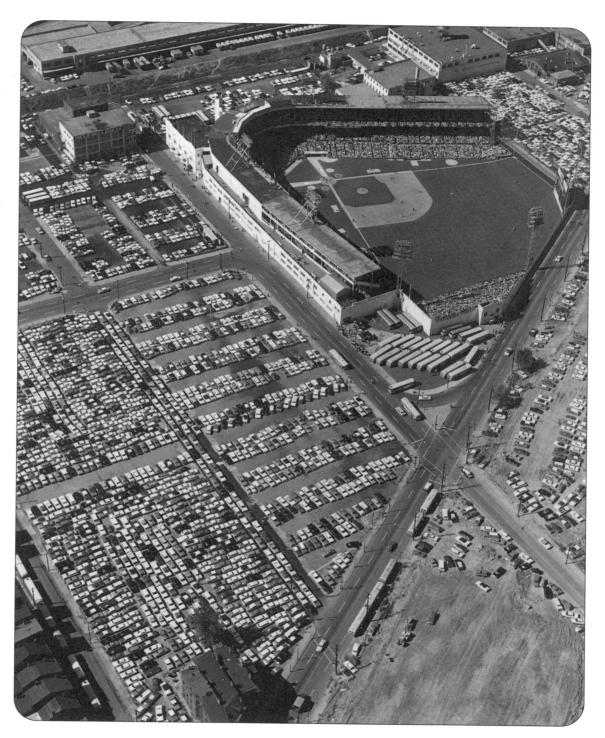

This aerial shot of Crosley Field during the 1961 World Series may have been taken from the Goodyear blimp which hovered above Findlay and Western.

The attendance for each of the three games in Cincinnati in the 1961 World Series was 32,589.

Compared to vast Yankee Stadium, Crosley's dimensions and grandstands appeared puny. One New York writer called Crosley "a picturesque little country ball park."

The path for the Millcreek Expressway (known as I-75 today) had been cut through the West End behind Crosley Field. But no work occurred during the series; the construction zone became a long-distance bleacher site.

Hundreds of fans gathered on the dirt embankment and sat on the roofs of their trucks and cars to peer over the center field fence. Several stood in a bulldozer scoop that had been raised high in the air.

Crosley Field

Left: *Roger Maris (left) broke Babe Ruth's home run record with 61 homers in 1961, and Mickey Mantle hit 54. They were expected to dominate Reds pitching, but Mantle was recovering from a hip abscess and only played in two games, going 1 for 6. Maris went just 2 for 19, but one hit was his dramatic ninth-inning home run into the Sun Deck in game three.*

Above: *The Reds and the Yankees lined up for pre-game ceremonies. The '61 Yankees are recognized as one of the great teams in baseball, winning 109 regular season games and hitting a major league record 240 home runs. Whitey Ford set a World Series record at Crosley Field when he passed Babe Ruth's mark of 29 2/3 consecutive scoreless innings.*

The Yankees left fielder, John Blanchard, a substitute starter for the ailing Mickey Mantle, hit a first-inning home run off Joey Jay in game five of the 1961 World Series, giving the Yankees a 2-0 lead. Before the inning was over, the Yankees had scored five runs and sent Jay to the showers. New York eventually won 13-5 and took the series, 4-1.

On the field for the Reds were Gordy Coleman (1b), Don Blasingame (2b), Eddie Kasko (ss), Gene Freese (3b), Johnny Edwards (c), and Jay.

The Saturday-Sunday-Monday games in Cincinnati drew standing-room-only crowds. Photographers, newsreel camera operators, and security people stood on the roof of the left field grandstand.

Crosley Field

With the way the Reds played on the field, most fans were probably happy to hear the diversion of music in the stands. Several Dixieland bands and German bands toured Crosley Field, playing "Charge" for the Reds, and "Taps" whenever a Yankee struck out or a pitcher was removed.

If the action on the field didn't please the fans, they could feast on 4,000 pounds of bratwurst and German sausage. They could wash it down with the 100,000 bottles of beer or 60,000 cups of lemonade. And if they didn't get enough to eat at the ballpark, they could buy some barbecue from one of the sidewalk vendors on the streets around Crosley.

Mel Allen interviewed a none-too-happy Fred Hutchinson after the final game of the 1961 World Series in the Yankees dressing room. Elston Howard, the Yankees catcher, stood by.

In addition to the game coverage provided by NBC, Ted Kluszewski and Bill Albert hosted a 30-minute pre-game show for WLW radio and television. Cincinnati radio coverage also included Waite Hoyt broadcasting play-by-play on WKRC.

This series, played at the height of Cold War tensions between the U.S. and the U.S.S.R. created satirical opportunities for some

writers with the use of the names, "Reds" and "Yanks." A Pennsylvania Supreme Court jurist, however, thought it was repugnant that Cincinnati had a baseball team named after the "brutal Bolshevistic gang." The judge feared that such headlines as "Reds Murder Yanks" would affect the nation's morale, and urged the club to change its name.

General Manager Bill DeWitt brushed the suggestion aside, noting that Powel Crosley liked the name Reds, and "if that's the name he wanted, it's good enough for me."

Crosley Field

Pete Takes the Field

By watching St. Louis Cardinals outfielder Enos "Country" Slaughter at Crosley Field, Pete Rose decided as a boy how he would play the game.

Slaughter ran all-out: to first base on routine groundouts, to the dugout from the outfield, and to the bank with his World Series checks.

Rose's dad, also named Pete, took him to games at Crosley Field as a toddler; later, Pete rode the bus to Crosley with his friends. Decades later, he could still remember the name of the busdriver. "Harry Hackman," said Rose, as though recalling a 3-2 pitch from yesterday.

Hackman liked Rose. He'd chauffeur the boy and his fellow west-side river-rat friends to the games for free. They'd yell out the windows at the fans going to the game.

"When I was a a kid, and my dad couldn't get to Crosley Field," said Rose, "I'd hang around outside. Skinny little crewcut kid and I'd go up to strangers and say, 'Got an extra ticket, mister?' Sometimes it worked. Sometimes I got into the ballpark that way."

Rose noticed the way heads-up runners usually got the extra base. When Rose met Jackie Robinson after Robinson had already retired from the game, Rose told him: "My father used to take me to Crosley Field to watch you play. I really enjoyed that. I loved the way you ran the bases."

From dust we came, and to dust we shall return. The difference between Pete Rose and the rest of us is the dust he raised in between. For Rose, raising dust as a Cincinnati Red began on Opening Day at Crosley Field in 1963.

Rose walked to the plate to the cheers of the hometown crowd.

With his spring-training hustle and pair of doubles in an extra-inning game, Rose had displaced popular veteran Don Blasingame at second base. Rose was the first local kid to start for the Reds since pitcher Herm Wehmeier in 1954. The first pitch from Pittsburgh Pirate Earl Francis was on its way.

Rose, as was his habit from his playground days when he would watch the ball from the pitcher's hand all the way back to the eye of the giant walleye mural (it was the strike zone on the side of the wall at Schulte's Fish Garden), followed Francis' pitch into the catcher's glove. Rose then looked veteran umpire Jocko Conlan right in the eye. Conlan called the pitch a ball and stepped out in front of the plate to dust it off and have a word with the rookie.

"What are you looking at kid?" asked Conlan.

"What? What?" responded a puzzled Rose.

"Why are turning around like that?" said Conlan. "If you want to know if it's a strike or ball, look out at the scoreboard."

"But I always look back," said Rose.

"Not when I'm behind the plate," said Conlan.

Rose took three more balls that first at-bat. Then, he took off for first base exactly like the "scalded dog" his minor-league manager Johnny Vander Meer had described. The fans howled their delight and Rose, for the first time since coming to the plate, smiled. Frank Robinson hit a towering home run, and Rose raced home, scoring his first major-league run.

"I'll never forget waiting there at home plate for Frank," said Rose. "It was like being a bit player in the greatest movie ever made."

Rose loved Robinson and his buddy, Vada Pinson, because the black outfielders befriended him when the white players wouldn't; they were upset that Rose had taken Blasingame's job. Rose splashed on their brand of cologne, wore his baseball pants long and tight like them, warmed up with them on the field before the game. The Reds' front office told Rose to stop hanging around the blacks. "It's bad for your image," he was told. Rose ignored the advice, just as he ignored it when manager Fred Hutchinson passed along the same message from above. Johnny Temple said Hutchinson told him in 1964 to make sure of two things: that Rose didn't hang around with the black players and that Rose learned how to use a knife and fork when he ate.

In this historic photograph, from Opening Day, April 8, 1963, Pete Rose, the unknown 21-year-old rookie from Cincinnati's Western Hills High School, who would eventually become baseball's all-time hit leader, was about to take his first step on a major league field.

The 1963 Opening Day lineup included (from left) Johnny Edwards, Vada Pinson, Gordy Coleman (18) Tommy Harper, Pete Rose, Frank Robinson, and Gene Freese (12).

You could have stuck a fork in Rose on Opening Day, 1963. He went 0-for-3. By the time he stepped in against the Pirates Bob Friend three days later at Forbes Field in Pittsburgh, Rose was 0-for-12.

"I was trying to pitch him in with a fastball," said Friend. "But I got it over the plate. He went with the pitch, taking it into the left-field corner."

Rose roared around second and slid into third. A triple. Pinson singled him home.

Hutchinson benched Rose after a 3-for-23 start as a hitter, but Rose eventually won his position back. On May 3, 22-year-old Pete Rose and 34-year-old Hamilton Joe Nuxhall combined for a 6-0 victory at Crosley Field over the Stan Musial-led Cardinals, the league leaders. Rose slammed a home run to center field off Ernie Broglio. Writers from around the league invoked the names of Slaughter and Pepper Martin and Frankie Frisch to try to find a suitable comparison for Rose. The fans had a new favorite.

Rose was named National League Rookie of the Year.

Pete posed with manager Fred Hutchinson in July, 1964, when he received his 1963 Rookie of the Year award.

On September 29, 1966, he went 5-for-5 off Giants spitballer Gaylord Perry; and on the final day of the season at Crosley Field, before 27,000 fans, Rose went 1-for-4 with a double off the Giants' Ray Sadecki, to beat out the Pirates' Matty Alou for the batting title. On the last day of the 1968 season, he had slight lead in the batting race over the Pirates' Roberto Clemente. This game, too, was at Crosley Field.

"I'm in right field and the fans have their portable radios and they're shouting, 'Better get one Pete! Clemente got a hit! Better get one Pete! He got another one!' The fans were right. Clemente went 3-for-3 that day," said Rose, who had one remaining at-bat.

"What do I do?" Rose asked his buddy and teammate, Tommy Helms. "Lay one down," said Helms.

Which Rose did. "A blueprint," said manager Dave Bristol.

Rose had won himself another batting title, and finished second in the MVP balloting to St. Louis Cardinals pitcher Bob Gibson.

Rose lived up to his vow: He became the first non-slugger to earn $100,000 a year. He took the money…and ran.

On June 24, 1970, he hit the last triple in the history of Crosley Field, and ran right into the history books. ◆

One of baseball's most memorable moments, and one of the all-time crowd favorites at Crosley Field, was a Pete Rose headfirst slide.

New Lineup: John, Paul, George & Ringo

Ever since Redland/Crosley Field opened in 1912, the ballpark had served as a venue for concerts and other events, but the most famous non-baseball act to appear there was the Beatles in 1966.

The British quartet made their first visit to the Queen City in 1965, playing at the 8,000-seat Cincinnati Gardens. The next summer local promoters booked Crosley Field, anticipating a crowd of 25,000 or more. The show was scheduled for Saturday night, August 20. Most grandstand tickets were priced at $5.50.

Advance ticket sales, however, were light and then threatening weather held walk-up sales to a minimum. But police still reported that by early evening of the concert, streets within a half mile of Crosley were jammed with cars, most filled with teen-aged girls. Many cars carried out-of-state plates, including one from Florida.

But instead of music, the crowd sat through two hours of thunder and rain before the concert was finally called off. The promoters considered cancelling the event, but the Beatles agreed to stay over an extra night and play an early Sunday show at noon before leaving for a Sunday night concert in St. Louis.

Many who had tickets to the Saturday show were unable to

The Beatles' stage was placed over second base. Stormy, humid weather and a last-minute postponement kept the crowd under 15,000.

return on Sunday. "How can I?" one girl wailed. "I'm going to church tomorrow."

The last-minute rescheduling also gave promoters little time to sell additional tickets. The result was a small Sunday crowd that the police estimated between 10 and 15,000.

Despite the thick humidity and high temperatures of the mid-August afternoon, the Sunday show went off as scheduled. Four acts provided 90 minutes of warm-up music (the Cyrkle, the Remains, the Ronettes, and Bobby Herb), and then the Beatles played a 30 minute show, featuring several songs from their recently-released movie, "Help!"

The "screaming youngsters," as the *Enquirer* characterized the crowd, were enthusiastic and well-behaved. Homemade banners hung from the grandstand railings. One read, "Beatles, We Luv Ya;" another read "Hi Ringo." Police reported only two minor incidents: a young boy and a girl hopped the low fence and ran on the field, but they were promptly returned to the stands.

At the conclusion of the concert, the Beatles, waving back at the crowd, were rushed to a gate in center field and into waiting automobiles on Western Avenue. The decision to play on Sunday and avoid the cancellation was worth $75,000 to the Beatles, according to an *Enquirer* estimate. ◆

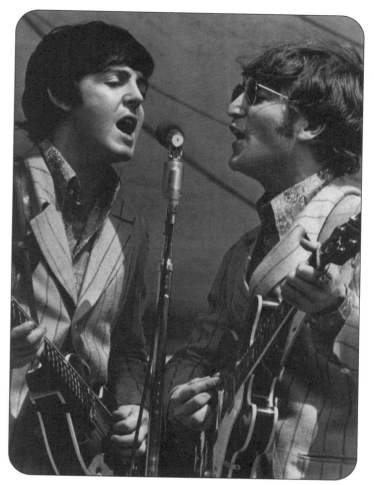

Above: *Paul McCartney (left) and John Lennon (right) entertained the crowd at Crosley Field in their 1966 Cincinnati concert. In the weeks prior to the concert, Lennon stirred up quite a controversy when he said the Beatles were more popular than Christianity. Ringo Starr thought that might have had some impact on the small Cincinnati crowd.*

"I don't think what John said bothered the fans," mused Ringo. "But we've lost audiences, you see, because their Mums and Dads pay for the tickets."

Left: *Thousands of screaming fans filled the Crosley grandstand. These teenagers, or their "Mums and Dads," paid $5.50 for the tickets.*

The Voice of Crosley Bids Farewell

From 1942 through 1965, Waite Hoyt, one of the most beloved personalities in Cincinnati sports, broadcast the games of the Reds.

On sunny days, and particularly on rainy days, Hoyt's crisp play-by-play and and fascinating anecdotes traveled over the Burger Beer baseball network across five states. Hoyt became synonymous with the Reds. "Waite's on," you'd say. "The Reds are on," you meant.

Hoyt, the Brooklyn native and ace of the 1920s New York Yankees pitching staff, pitched into the late 1930s. Unlike many ballplayers of the time, Hoyt was well-spoken and had obvious talents beyond the playing field. After his retirement in 1938, he turned to radio. He wanted to be the Yankees play-by-play announcer, but they never gave him a serious audition; in that era of the classically-trained announcer, an ex-baseball player had two strikes against him.

Hoyt did pre-game shows and sports commentary, but he longed for a play-by-play job and when Cincinnati's WKRC held auditions for an announcer in the winter of 1941, Hoyt sent them a recording. Two other Cincinnati stations already carried the Reds, but Burger Beer wanted to expand its market and teamed up with WKRC. Hoyt was their first choice.

In the book, *Voices of the Game*, Hoyt recalled hearing from WKRC. "When they offered me the job of play-by-play, it took me about half a second to yell 'yes.' Originally, I'd had a few qualms about going; after all, Cincinnati was the only place in the majors that closed down after dark. But I went and, when I did, I found a level of happiness I'd never known anywhere else, young or old."

Hoyt had reason to note Cincinnati's staid reputation, for he was a heavy drinker, an alcoholic. In the summer of 1945, after a broadcast, he failed to come home. His wife reported him missing, and the newspapers ran front page stories. "Waite Hoyt Reported Missing; Amnesia Sufferer, Wife Says," headlined the *Enquirer*.

Hoyt returned home the next day, recovered from his "amnesia," but a few weeks later he privately and publicly admitted he was an alcoholic. It was a necessary revelation, but with potentially serious consequences. Could a beer company continue to employ an admitted alcoholic as its spokesperson? If Burger had any serious questions, they were soon answered by the massive public support Waite received.

The fans loved Waite for his straight-forward reporting, as well as his knowledge of baseball history and his obvious relish at telling stories. During rain delays, Waite would reminisce about his career, about the legends he had known. The tales became so popular, Burger released two recordings of Waite's rain stories. On one, he recalled pitching a game for the Philadelphia Athletics in 1931. The story seemed over, but then he turned to his broadcast partner, Jack Moran, and said, "If Moran would be so kind as to ask what happened else in that game, why I'd be very happy to answer him."

"What happened," asked Moran, as Hoyt began to chuckle.

"I got three hits!" he said and his laughter continued to build. "Including a double….Boom! Off that fence. And I tell you that fence shook just like…a missile hit it. The fact of the matter is the ground crew ran out there, it took 'em three days to repair that wall…."

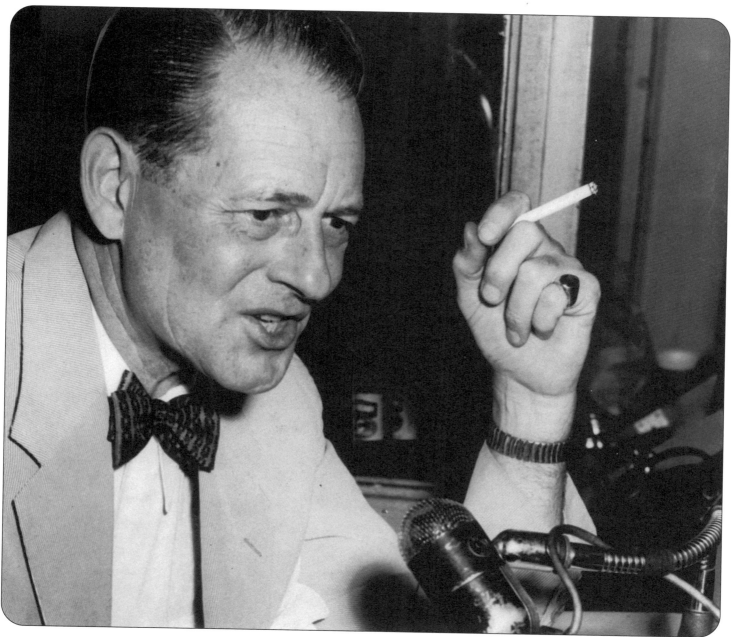

Waite Hoyt broadcast from the press box atop the grandstand at Crosley, and one of his greatest moments came in August, 1948, when he received word that Babe Ruth had died. Hoyt asked his listeners to stay tuned after the game and he would say a few words about his old teammate.

The few words turned into a two-hour, heartfelt eulogy, both sad and funny, as Waite recalled the game's greatest player in a classic ad-lib radio broadcast.

Crosley Field

But Hoyt had his hard edge, a commitment to calling the game as a reporter, not as a cheerleader. In his book, *Pennant Race*, Jim Brosnan recalled a game in 1961 when reliever Jim Maloney gave up four runs. When a late Reds rally fell short, Hoyt let the fans know where he placed the blame.

"If Hutchinson had a little pitching today, the Reds would still be in the game. Those four runs Maloney gave up look mighty big."

Maloney, who was listening in the clubhouse, threw his wet sweatshirt at the radio and said, "That second guessing old s.o.b.!" he yelled. "I guess he could do any better."

Hoyt probably could have. He made the Hall of Fame in 1969 for his pitching career, and he also could have been inducted in the broadcast wing as well. His 23 years with Burger Beer and the Reds was one of the longest streaks any broadcaster has ever had with one club. But, then, Reds fans have grown accustomed to such longevity. The "Old Lefthander" Joe Nuxhall, who began his broadcasting career in 1967 at Crosley Field, has topped Hoyt.

For the record, Hoyt had four partners: Lee Allen, Jack Moran, Gene Kelly, and Claude Sullivan, and he broadcast on four stations: WKRC, WSAI, WCPO, and WCKY. ◆

After his retirement from broadcasting, Hoyt briefly considered running for city council, but never entered politics. He spent much of his time with a new avocation: painting. Above he worked on a view of Crosley Field in the 1950s. Hoyt died in1984.

Waite Hoyt bade the Cincinnati fans farewell in 1965. Hoyt ended his broadcast career somewhat prematurely that year when Burger Beer gave up its sponsorship of baseball. The new sponsor wanted Hoyt to continue, but Waite refused out of his long-association with Burger. After all, his listeners had grown accustomed to home runs at Crosley landing in "Burgerville."

Crosley Field

Jim Maloney: "As Good as Koufax"

For most pitchers, Crosley Field was a crib too cozy for comfort.

"If I pitched here," said Dodgers' pitcher Don Drysdale, "I wouldn't have a winning record."

But, for Jim Maloney, Crosley Field was a pitcher's playpen. In his seven full seasons with the Reds, Maloney's record from 1963 through 1969 was a whopping 57 games over .500. He won two of every three games (117-60) in which he got decisions.

His .661 winning percentage was 130 points higher than the Reds overall record (.531) during the same stretch. That is called rising above it.

Maloney was the the most dominating pitcher in the history of Crosley Field. He pitched three no-hitters, two of them at Crosley, the first a 10-inning affair which he lost, 1-0, in the 11th against the New York Mets on June 14, 1965, when .250-hitting Johnny Lewis hit a 2-1 fastball five feet over the yellow line on the center field wall for a home run.

"That one was a heartbreaker," said former teammate Joe Nuxhall. "Jim struck out 18 guys that night. When he was on, nobody ever threw a baseball better than Jim Maloney – and I mean nobody."

Two months after losing to the Mets in the 11th, Maloney no-hit the Cubs in Wrigley Field and won, 1-0, behind the 10th-inning home run of Leo Cardenas. Maloney also threw two one-hitters that year. Despite being 23-7 in 1963 and 20-9 in 1965, Maloney was known as a hard-luck pitcher, primarily because of the 11th-inning loss to the Mets. The Maloney family's coat of arms, wrote columnist Jim Murray, should be "a field of black cats rampant on a shield of snake-eyed dice."

Maloney holds Reds records for career strikeouts (1,592), for strikeouts in a nine-inning game (16), and for strikeouts in an extra-inning game (18). In 1965, Maloney's fastball was clocked at 99.5 miles per hour, faster than anybody else's of that era and only imperceptibly slower than Nolan Ryan's five years later.

"Maloney had such a great fastball and curve that he was unhittable if he got them both over," said former teammate, Jim O'Toole. "He was as good as (Sandy) Koufax."

On a few, rare occasions Maloney enhanced his repertoire with a Vaseline ball, the spitball of the 1960s, the lubricant mixed secretly with the sweat on his body, most likely on the back of his neck. After he was out of baseball, he all but confirmed that he threw a spitter.

In addition to these "prank" pitches, Maloney also specialized in pranks of the clubhouse variety, such as lighting his teammates' shoelaces on fire. But Maloney was not kidding when he smeared his arm with a red-hot salve called "Atomic Balm." "I don't know how he stood it," said Nuxhall. "He said it kept his arm loose."

After Maloney's third career no-hitter, Reds president Bob Howsam (left) cheerfully added a bonus to Jim's contract.

Maloney had his best stuff the night of April 30, 1969, taking a no-hitter into the ninth against the Houston Astros at Crosley Field. The Houston Astros' first hitter in the ninth was Joe Morgan. He flied out to Pete Rose. After another out and a walk, Maloney faced Dave Rader.

Johnny Bench, who was normally Mr. Calm, was behind the plate. ("He'll come out to the mound and chew me out as if I were a 2-year-old," said Maloney.) But in the eighth inning, Bench stood and clapped when Maloney came to bat. By the ninth inning, Bench was really feeling the unfamiliarity of the territory.

"He was so nervous his fingers were shaking as he gave the sign," said Maloney. "I didn't know whether to tell him to cool it."

Moments later Maloney had his 13th strikeout and his third no-hitter was in the books. Only Koufax and Bob Feller were in there with him.

The only thing standing between Maloney and Cooperstown was the Achilles tendon he tore on April 16, 1970, when he sprang from the batter's box at Crosley Field to run out a ground ball. The injury, for all practical effect, ended his career at 32.

Years later, Maloney looked back on his career with great memories. "I feel very fortunate I pitched in an era where I got to pitch against Koufax and Gibson and Marichal," said Maloney. "I was lucky in a lot of ways." ◆

Johnny Bench celebrated with the final pitch of Jim Maloney's third no-hitter on April 30, 1969, before 6,157 fans at Crosley Field. Maloney said Bench was so nervous, his fingers shook when he gave the signs. The next night, Don Wilson of the Astros, no-hit the Reds.

Building a Big Red Machine

The Big Red Machine era in Cincinnati baseball will always be linked to the 1970s and Riverfront Stadium, but the team and the nickname itself were born at Crosley Field.

Three of the greatest stars of what was to become one of baseball's greatest teams, joined the Reds in the 1960s. Pete Rose debuted for the Reds in 1963 and Tony Perez won a starting job at third base in 1965. Three years later, Johnny Bench became the starting catcher, and like Rose and Tommy Helms won a Rookie of the Year Award.

Five of the eight starters on the 1970 team, the first of the Big Red Machine era, started for the 1968 club: Lee May, Tommy Helms, Tony Perez, Pete Rose, and Johnny Bench.

The nickname which was to so aptly characterize the power and domination of the Reds in the 1970s was first used in 1969. According to Bob Hertzel, author of the book, *The Big Red Machine*, both Pete Rose and Bob Hunter of the Los Angeles *Herald-Examiner* claimed they originated the term, Big Red Machine. Perhaps both were right.

Rose said he began using the name around Crosley Field to describe the club as a comparison to a red, 1934 Ford he owned. "That, I said, was the Little Red Machine and the team was the Big Red Machine," remembered Rose.

But it took the power of the press, through the writing of Hunter, to give the term public appeal. Hunter said he never heard anyone use the term, he just hung the nickname on the Reds after they won a slugfest with the Phillies, 19-17. When Cincinnati came to LA, Hunter wrote of the march of the Big Red Machine. Other papers soon picked it up and the club even copyrighted the name. The term first appeared in an official Reds publication in the 1970 program when Hertzel reviewed the 1969 year under the headline "The Big Red Machine."

In 1967, Bob Howsam replaced Bill DeWitt as general manager of the club, and became the executive vice-president as well. He brought with him a reputation as an aggressive trader, and in the next two seasons, fans at Crosley watched the club bring in Bobby Tolan, Jim Merritt, Tony Cloninger, Clay Carroll, Woody Woodward, Wayne Granger, and Jim McGlothlin, who helped create the first edition of the Big Red Machine and lead the club to the 1970 World Series. ◆

Above: *On Opening Day, April 7, 1969, at Crosley Field, Pete Rose hit the first pitch of the season into the screen over the left field wall to give the Reds a 1-0 lead over Don Drysdale and the Dodgers. The next batter, Bobby Tolan also followed with a home run, but the Reds eventually lost the opener, 3-2.*

Rose was greeted (from left) by Alex Johnson (29), Woody Woodward, Tony Perez, Johnny Bench, trainer Bill Cooper, and Ted Savage (20).

In this first season of divisional play, the Reds challenged the Braves and the Giants for the National League West title, but finished third.

Left: *Johnny Bench, a new home plate in hand, posed for Cincinnati Post photographer Jack Klumpe at the Riverfront Stadium site in 1968 upon the announcement that Bench had won the Rookie of the Year Award.*

The 1969 Reds watched the lowering of the flag to half-mast on Opening Day in memory of former president, Dwight D. Eisenhower. The 1969 Reds included several stars of the Big Red Machine era, including Johnny Bench (5), Pete Rose (14), Tommy Helms (19), Lee May (23), Tony Perez (24), Bobby Tolan (28), Jim Merritt (30), Clay Carroll (36), and Gary Nolan (38).

By the late 1960s, the Reds uniforms had also taken on a look consistent with the Big Red Machine era. Although the club was not yet wearing the double-knit fabric uniform (that began in1972), they had abandoned the sleeveless vest and pinstripes (worn since the mid-1950s), switched from white to red caps, and placed names on the back of the uniforms (a practice begun in 1966).

Crosley Field 191

The Ninth

1970 and Beyond: Long Live Crosley

Demolition crews removed the seats in Crosley Field in 1972. Many seats were acquired by individuals as mementos, and have become valuable collector's items.

A FTER NEARLY A DECADE OF WRANGLING ABOUT IF, WHEN, AND WHERE A new ballpark would be built in Cincinnati, the issue was finally resolved in a series of decisions in 1966. One of the most crucial was the awarding of an National Football League franchise to Cincinnati, and the subsequent agreement between the Reds and the Bengals to share a new stadium. In 1967 the Reds and the Bengals signed 40-year leases, and by mid-1967, construction had begun.

Although the progress of the stadium drew considerable public attention and news coverage, the facility remained nameless. Opinion polls by the local press discovered sentiment for a variety of namesakes: Taft, Eisenhower, Rhodes (for Governor James Rhodes), Powel Crosley, Fred Hutchinson, and Neil Armstrong. Other proposed names included Regal Stadium, Queen City Stadium, Riverbank, Buckeye Bowl, and the to-the-point Red/Bengal Stadium. Finally the unofficial name the project had carried since it was first proposed became official: Riverfront Stadium.

Regardless of the official name, for most of the late 1960s, people called the stadium "expensive" and "delayed." In 1965, a new stadium was priced at $20 million. By 1966, estimates reached $43 million, and the final bill was $52 million, with most of the money raised by county revenue bonds. The original construction timetable called for the stadium to open in 1967, but the date was pushed back to August of 1968, then to 1969, then to the beginning of the 1970 season, and finally to June 30, 1970 which proved to be the actual opening.

At the final game at Crosley Field on June 24, 1970, veteran photographer Gene Smith, who estimated he had seen 2,200 games at Crosley, said, "I hate to see the old place go. Before you know it, it'll be like it never existed." As it turned out, Crosley did come tumbling down, but Smith need not have worried about civic memories failing. Since June 25, 1970, the story of Crosley is not one of a memory lost, but of a dream reborn. ◆

By early 1969, Riverfront Stadium had taken shape, its circular shell of steel and concrete rising above the Ohio River.

When Crosley Field was built in 1912, it was part of a national trend that saw 11 parks built from 1909 to 1914. When Crosley was abandoned in 1970, it was again due, in part, to a national trend, this time towards round, symmetrical, multi-purpose facilities for both baseball and football. Whereas the original building frenzy produced intimate, distinctive, neighborhood parks, the boom of the 1960s-70s produced impersonal, uniform, regional stadia, sometimes domed and often with Astroturf.

Three of the "concrete doughnuts" opened in 1970: Riverfront, Three Rivers in Pittsburgh, and Veterans Stadium in Philadelphia.

Crosley Field

The Last Opening Day

Before the last set of delays in the construction of Riverfront Stadium, it appeared that the final game at Crosley Field would be at the end of the 1969 season, but Opening Day, 1970, found the Reds at the familiar Findlay and Western location.

Two soon-to-be-familiar Reds were introduced to the crowd this day, shortstop David Concepcion and manager George "Sparky" Anderson.

Despite gloomy, wet weather, the first fans arrived at the ballpark before noon for the 2:30 start. They jostled for the best autograph positions along the railings of the grandstands as the players came out to inspect the field. Intermittent rain cancelled batting practice.

At 1 o'clock, the Findlay Market Association parade began at Elder Street, and headed toward Crosley Field. When the Findlay Market merchants first organized a parade in 1920, to honor the 1919 World Series champions, they were just one of several groups to parade to the ballpark. But the Findlay Market group consistently put on the biggest and most enthusiastic show, and by the 1930s, they became the official organizer of the Opening Day festivities.

By 1970, the 50th anniversary of the parade, the festivities included a queen ("Miss Findlay Market Baseball Queen"), and the formal presentation of a United States flag to fly over the ballpark during the season.

The opening ceremonies were conducted under an ever-darkening sky, but even the sun knew when to make an appearance at Opening Day, especially the final opener at Crosley Field. Game time was 2:30; the sun popped through the clouds at 2:29.

The Reds faced the Montreal Expos in the April 6 opener, the earliest date the opener had ever been played. The Big Red Machine, or "La Grande Machine Rouge" as the Expos announcers put it, scored four runs in the fourth (three on a Lee May home run) and Jim Merritt pitched a complete game, 5-1 victory.

The Reds made the most of the eleven-week reprieve Crosley had been given by the construction delay, winning 17 of their first 21 games at home. The club's only day out of first place all season was after a loss in San Francisco. Crosley Field never saw second place in its final year.

The Reds won every way possible at Crosley. On April 17, Hal McRae and Tony Perez hit ninth-inning home runs to beat the Giants, 8-5. On June 7, Johnny Bench drove in five runs to lead a 10-2 rout of the Mets. Rookie Wayne Simpson pitched a one hitter against the Giants on April 19. On May 1, Sparky Anderson moved pitcher Wayne Granger to left field for one batter so he could return Granger to the mound; the Reds won 6-4 over the Pirates.

The one moment of anguish came on April 16 when Jim Maloney, 29, ruptured his achilles tendon. Maloney had just hit a ground ball and pivoted to run to first base when the injury occurred. Maloney, who won 134 games for the Reds in the 1960s, would never win another game. Ironically, rookie Don Gullett, who would assume Maloney's crown as the most dominating Cincinnati pitcher, relieved Maloney and won his first game.

One of baseball's milestone moments occurred on May 17 when Hank Aaron made his 3,000 hit on an infield grounder. Stan Musial was on hand to help Aaron celebrate. Undaunted, the Reds won the game in 15 innings. ◆

George "Sparky" Anderson, one of the most successful managers in baseball history made his major league debut on April 6, 1970. His managerial opponent was Montreal's Gene Mauch.

When the virtually unknown Anderson was hired by Bob Howsam in October of 1969 to replace the popular Dave Bristol, the press greeted the announcement with "Sparky Who?" headlines. Anderson had never managed a major league team. He was just 36 years old.

Visible on the scoreboard behind Anderson, was a horizontal line that matched the height of the center field wall. The club painted this line on the scoreboard in 1969. Any ball hit above the line was a home run. The '69 and '70 seasons were the only years in the history of Crosley Field that a ball hitting the scoreboard could be a home run. For the previous 56 seasons, the entire scoreboard had always been in play.

Farewell Crosley

Finally, after 4,543 games it was time to go.

The Reds and the Giants were scheduled for a night game on Wednesday, June 24, 1970. After a brief road trip, the Reds next home game was set for June 30 against the Braves. That would be the first game at the new Riverfront Stadium. Cincinnati was ready; civic enthusiasm for the shiny new stadium was overwhelming.

But on Wednesday, June 24, the people came to pay one last visit to its old friend at Findlay and Western. The club hired extra police, but there were no incidents. As *Enquirer* reporter Bob Hertzel said, "It was a happy wake."

It was a night for memories, for one last round of stories, the last chance for an older generation to take a younger one in hand and say, "This is the way it was." One gentleman carried a scorecard from 1912. Another had a photo of himself ushering in 1918. Pete Rose had a old Crosley memory: "I even got a foul ball here when I was a kid. It came on one bounce and I caught it. You can't imagine how proud I was."

The park wasn't quite full at 28,027, but then they had to leave room for the memories of Roush and Groh and 1919, of Rixey and Larry MacPhail and night baseball, of Walters, Derringer, and Lombardi, of Vandy, of Hutchinson and the Ragamuffins of '61, of Hoyt and Barber and Matty Schwab. And a thousand others.

But even on this night there were mixed feelings about the old orchard. No doubt many were relieved that this was the last time they would have to fight the parking nightmare of the crowded West End streets. Someone surely mentioned that there would be no more pillars to block the view at Riverfront.

In an era familiar with public demonstrations, there were no protestors outside Crosley lamenting its demise. No, after 4,543 games, and 58 seasons, it was time to go.

Players too, were ready for the move. "Crosley had fabulous character," Johnny Bench recalled. "But boy was it miserable and mushy out there when it rained." Tommy Harper who played outfield in the mid-1960s, spoke for many players when he admitted he wouldn't miss the terrace. "I often asked myself, as I was getting up off the ground, why they had it."

But before they called in the wrecking ball, the Reds and the Giants had one last game to play, and it was a classic.

The lead changed three times in seven innings. Giants led 1-0, Reds led 2-1, Giants led 4-3, and going into the bottom of the eighth, it appeared that the Crosley era would conclude on a losing note. The first two hitters in the eighth were Bench and Lee May. The pitcher was Juan Marichal.

"Come on and get on Johnny," said May to Bench. "Let me be a hero."

"I almost turned around and said why don't we both hit one out," said Bench.

Bench delivered, tying the game with a shot over the left field wall, and May followed with a home run to center field. The Reds won, 5-4.

It was time to go, but nobody wanted to leave. Ronnie Dale, the organist, and singer Marian Spelman entertained the hangers-on with the traditional closing songs and the fans sang with them: "Auld Lang Syne," "God Bless America," and "Good Night Sweetheart."

Long after 11, long after the game had ended, the last fans finally filed out. ◆

At 10:44 on June 24, 1970, Wayne Granger delivered the final pitch in the history of Crosley Field to Bobby Bonds of the San Francisco Giants.

Moments before, in the eighth inning, Johnny Bench and Lee May had hit back to back home runs to put the Reds ahead in a storybook ending. Reds radio announcer Jim McIntyre, with more than a little help from his partner, Joe Nuxhall, called the final Crosley homer:

"Johnny Bench's home run has just tied it at 4–4, and Mr. Marichal has now allowed the Reds nine hits, and we've got a brand-new ball game here in the eighth inning. Two and two to May. On deck, Bernie Carbo....Now the pitch. Swung on, a high drive, deep center field!" In the background, Nuxhall shouted, "Get outa here, outa here, babe get outa here! I tell ya, out, out, outa here!" McIntyre finished: "...its over the center-field fence! A home run for Lee May! And the Reds have taken the lead, 5–4."

Granger made quick work of the Giants in the ninth, retiring Bonds himself on an easy grounder back to the mound for the last out. Others in the photograph included Bench (c), Tony Perez (3b), Darryl Chaney (ss), and Carbo (lf). Tito Fuentes was on deck.

Crosley Field

After the final out and after the players had left the field for the last time, the grounds crew dug up home plate and presented it to Mayor Gene Ruehlmann. Ruehlmann, who played a critical role in the development of Riverfront Stadium, climbed aboard a helicopter and took the plate a mile and one-half south to its new home at Riverfront.

In ceremonies after the game, the club raffled off the bases to three fans. Many others leaned over the grandstand railings and scooped up handfuls of sacred Crosley dirt into cups and even caps. The Crosley Field memorabilia craze had just begun.

Eventually after the ceremonies and the songs, the lights dimmed and the fans left, except for Frank O'Toole. The Cincinnati native walked around the stands. He grabbed a handful dirt and put it in a cup. He

shimmied up a beam and grabbed the "Press" sign over the media entrance for a souvenir. He even helped the clean-up crew with a couple of tasks.

But, finally, he too had to leave. Fifty-eight years earlier, a youngster named Mike Maxwell had been the first fan through the gates at the new Redland Field. Now, Frank O'Toole would be the last to walk out.

"I didn't plan to be the last," said O'Toole. "I just kind of hated to leave."

Crosley Field

Final Days

From 1970–1972, the City of Cincinnati used Crosley Field as an impoundment lot.

Part of the complex negotiations surrounding the move from Crosley Field to Riverfront Stadium involved the future of Crosley Field. The City of Cincinnati had agreed to buy the old ballpark, with the goal of creating an industrial park on the site. But, determining a price for Crosley became a point of contention, and the city and the Reds wound up in court in 1969.

The Reds valued the eight acres of land and the structures at $3.5 million, while the city countered with an offer of $1.5 million.

The city called witnesses who claimed Crosley was obsolete with little value as a ballfield. An expert appraiser testified that the major items of obsolescence at Crosley Field were the bleachers, the scoreboard, the raised outfield terrace, the pillars in the grandstands, and the lack of parking lots. No stadium built in the 1970s would have any of these characteristics. In addition, the field itself would have to be extensively reworked to prepare it for industrial buildings. Some parts of the field were 11 feet below the surrounding streets.

The Cincinnati Reds, Inc. countered with their own expert witness: Peter Edward Rose. After establishing his qualifications as an expert on ballparks (he was paid $55,000 in 1968 to play professional baseball), Rose declared, "Personally, I'd rather play in Crosley Field than in any other park." Rose said he rated Crosley's infield and outfield as better than at most other fields. "There are not as many bad hops."

Another witness for the club, an engineer, estimated that it would cost $4.5 million to replace Crosley Field Eventually, the jury decided the worth of Crosley at $2.5 million.

Although the city gained title to the park when the Reds left in the middle of the 1970 season, the industrial park project, part of a larger effort known as Queensgate, was not ready. Rather than let their investment sit idle, the city turned the ballpark into an impoundment lot for abandoned and unclaimed autos. Cars, oil stains, and weeds soon covered the once-pristine turf.

By April 1972, the cars were removed from the lot, and the city prepared the site for demolition. The city began salvaging the seats, selling them to organizations and individuals. Price: $10 each.

Relics and mementos, ranging from the scoreboard to single bricks from the grandstand walls were purchased or retrieved by souvenir hunters. Former business manager John Murdough and Bill DeWitt, Jr. found a plaque honoring Matty Schwab in the trash, retrieved it, and returned it to the Schwab family.

On April 19, Pete Rose, Jr. sat in a crane and pulled the switch that sent the wrecking ball into the bulls-eye of the Reds centennial logo on the right field bleacher wall. By the fall of 1972, Crosley Field had disappeared. ◆

The main grandstand behind home plate fell in the summer of 1972. Souvenir hunters purchased and salvaged many relics during the demolition.

Above: *The center field wall was demolished and part of the grandstand destroyed in this photo taken in the summer of 1972, from across Western Avenue, where factory buildings once lined the street.*

Right: *After demolition was completed, the faint outline of the grandstand was the only evidence remaining that a ballpark once graced the corner of Findlay and Western.*

This view, looking west, is framed by Findlay Street on the south (left), York Street on the north, and Western Avenue and I-75 on the east. The Crosley Field scoreboard sat at the intersection of York and Western Avenue. The laundry was on the northwest corner of York and Western. Compare this view with the aerial photograph on page 7.

Crosley Field

A Queensgate Tribute to Crosley

The vast industrial park that eventually replaced much of the 19th-century housing stock in Cincinnati's West End was known as Queensgate. The northern edge of the development, which occupied the Crosley Field site and the surrounding area, was Queensgate North industrial park.

The Crosley site could not be developed, however, until it was filled. Dating back to 1884, when the first grandstand was erected on the old brickyard site, the playing field had always been depressed. The left field terrace was a natural phenomenon, an embankment created by the difference between street level and the level of the old brick yard. Any who walked into or out of the park from the Western Avenue gate in center field next to the scoreboard fence certainly remembered that. Fans had to walk down five steps from street level to reach the field, and that was the top of the terrace. The terrace then sloped another four feet to the main level of the outfield, and then there was a gradual slope towards home plate. Portions of the field around home plate were 11 feet below the level of Western Avenue.

The site was filled (although a part of the terrace rise remained along York Street), but businesses were slow to commit to the new development. The first business to move into Queensgate North was the Phillips Supply Co., which occupied the western end of Findlay Avenue in the fall of 1976. Crosley Field had been gone for four years, but in owner Charles Phillips' mind it was certainly not forgotten.

Phillips, who recalled going to games at Crosley Field beginning when he was a youngster, decided to create a monument to the old ballpark. Outside the main entrance to his new plant, he built a 12 by 16 foot scale model of the playing field, complete with infield and base lines. It was made of concrete and Astroturf, materials more at home in the new Riverfront Stadium than in old Crosley, but without Matty Schwab around, Phillips wanted to keep the maintenance simple. Surrounding the model were two rows of Crosley field seats salvaged from the park.

Artist Richard Skurow created a two-foot high painted backdrop that framed the outfield. The scene pictured Crosley in the 1950s, with the old scoreboard, the laundry behind left field, the factory buildings lining Western Avenue, and a crowded Sun Deck. Unfortunately, weather and vandalism later damaged the painted backdrop and it was removed.

Phillips also installed a bronze home plate, on the south side of his building, commemorating the site as the location of Crosley's home plate, although in fact, home plate in 1970 was located some 60 feet further north.

On April 19, 1977, the new building was dedicated, including the Crosley monuments. Waite Hoyt attended and reminisced about the ballpark. He remembered the bad: "The rain used to come up the steps of the broadcasting booth," he recalled. "The roof had a tar covering, but there was all kinds of metal. I used to wonder during the thunder and lightning if I'd end up as a lightning rod."

And the good: "Crosley Field was more intimate than Riverfront....Crosley Field was like the private sanctuary of the people of Cincinnati. It had intensity. You could feel the reactions and the pulsations of the crowd."

When the scale model was unveiled, Hoyt sat in one of the old Crosley seats, and wiped the tears from his eyes.

The official address of Phillips Supply Co. was 1230 Findlay Street. Phillips renamed it: "One Crosley Lane." ◆

Above: Prior to demolition in 1972, Crosley Field dominated the view from the corner of Findlay and Western as it had for 58 years. This view looked west, across Western Avenue. The right field bleachers were behind the sign "Crosley Field," and Findlay Street ran along the left edge of the grandstand.

Below: The same perspective, taken some 20 years later, pictured the Queensgate North development. Low-rise industrial buildings line Findlay Street and Western Avenue.

Crosley Field

The aerial views above and right illustrate the massive changes in the area around Crosley Field between 1962 and 1990, prior to the demolition of Crosley and after the development of Queensgate North. Both photographs look southwest towards the rail yards of the Millcreek Valley. Both photos include the path of I-75 (cleared, but not paved in the photo above), and the Dalton Street post office (one block south of Crosley).

The above photograph from June, 1990, showed seven buildings on the former Crosley Field site. The most significant streetscape change was the extension of Dalton Avenue, which dead-ended at Findlay in the Crosley era. Dalton was extended through what was once the right field grandstand, behind the infield and through the left field wall just west of the scoreboard to join the old Western Avenue.

Western Avenue originally continued parallel to I-75 behind the center field wall. The three buildings east of Dalton Street occupied center field, right field, and the Sun Deck of Crosley, while the four buildings west of Dalton, between Findlay and York, occupied the infield, left field, the grandstand and the parking lot just west of the old grandstand.

Crosley Resurrected

Hard by I-275 in the northern reaches of Cincinnati in the suburb of Blue Ash, stands a remarkable tribute to the force of memory and the lure of baseball. In 1988, the city of Blue Ash resurrected Crosley Field, opening a ballfield that featured the exact dimensions of Crosley, and a re-creation of the outfield wall and the 58 foot high scoreboard.

What makes the nostalgic power of Crosley even more impressive is that the Blue Ash project was the *second* revival of Crosley Field.

You just can't keep a good ballpark down.

During the demolition of Crosley in 1972, Larry Luebbers of Union, Kentucky, about 20 miles south of Cincinnati, went to the site to buy a couple of seats. But then he saw the scoreboard, the advertising signs, the foul poles, the dugouts and he settled on a plan to re-create Crosley on his farm.

By 1974, the outfield walls rose on the Kentucky landscape, framing a field that was built to Crosley's dimensions. The advertising signs were in place, the scoreboard partially rebuilt, and the dugouts were in the ground. Luebbers added seats, put up the concession signs and placards that he had salvaged and called the place Crosley Field. His professional softball team, the Cincinnati Suds, played games there, but by 1984, the Suds had collapsed and Luebbers faced financial difficulty. He sold his farm, including his Crosley Field and memorabilia.

What happened next is not clear, but it appears the new owners had no interest in saving the remains of an old ballpark. Crosley buffs who visited Union about this time found a sad site. The fences had been torn down; the field had deteriorated; many Crosley items had disappeared. Mike Shannon, writing in "Spitball" magazine said, "It is hard to believe, but it is true;

somehow, for some reason – or worse, for no reason – Crosley Field was demolished again." Luebbers later speculated, "I guessed they bulldozed it under."

But about the time the Kentucky Crosley died, the Blue Ash Crosley was born. Blue Ash was building a new recreation complex with several ballfields. City Manager Marvin Thompson, who as a child attended games at the real Crosley in the 1960s, wanted one of the fields to re-create Crosley's dimensions. The idea took seed, nourished by positive reaction and Thompson's drive, and soon a much more elaborate plan took shape. Why not put in the terrace, replicate the scoreboard, build some grandstands with Crosley seats? Thompson put administrative aide Mark Rohr in charge and sent him looking for Crosley memorabilia.

Rohr had heard of Luebbers' project and investigated the Union site, but received a very cool reception to his inquiries about Crosley artifacts. The only item salvaged from the Kentucky Crosley was a ticket booth, which Luebber's mother had removed from the farm and kept in her backyard.

But Rohr had much more success elsewhere, finding hundreds of original seats and the original plans for Crosley. As news of the project spread, people began donating Crosley Field items, including signs, a field microphone, rooftop pennants, usher's uniforms, and other memorabilia.

The Blue Ash Crosley opened in 1988 with an old-timer's game and has hosted one each year. The former players love it.

"It's beautiful," said Pete Rose.

"The first time I saw the way they had rebuilt the park," said Jim O'Toole, "I came very close to crying. There are so many memories there." ◆

The Union, Kentucky Crosley Field ground crew worked on Larry Luebber's field of dreams in 1975. Financial problems eventually forced Luebbers to sell his property and most of the Crosley artifacts disappeared. Luebbers believed the new owners, who had no interest in preserving Crosley simply "bulldozed it under."

Administrative aide Mark Rohr (left) and Jim Pfeffer, the executive director of administrative and recreational services posed before the replica of the Crosley Field scoreboard in Blue Ash. The information on the scoreboard matches exactly the details from the moment of the last pitch of June 24, 1970.

Rohr was responsible for researching the history of Crosley and salvaging Crosley memorabilia. Pfeffer admitted he was not a baseball fan before the project began and seemed bemused by the interest stirred up by the re-creation.

"Sometimes I have a hard time understanding the people who come and stare at this place with tears in their eyes. A woman actually hugged the ticket booth and kissed it."

The old-timers game at Crosley Field in Blue Ash annually features players from the Reds and other teams in a spirited contest, played before 5-6,000 fans. The field, which is meticulously manicured to a standard that would have pleased even Matty Schwab, also hosts Knothole leagues, a summer collegiate team, and is the home field for two high schools.

In addition, hundreds of Crosley nostalgia-seekers stop by each year, unannounced, to walk around the field, test the terrace, and touch the walls. "Scores of people stop by," said city manager Marvin Thompson. "They pull off the road and come in and walk around. It's Blue Ash's number one tourist attraction."

A Crosley Scrapbook

Crosley's Most Memorable Moments

October 8, 1940: The Reds win the 7th game of the World Series, coming from behind to defeat Detroit, 2-1.

September 28, 1939: Paul Derringer pitches a thrilling 5-3 victory over 2nd-place St. Louis to clinch the pennant.

May 24, 1935: Larry MacPhail and the Reds introduce night baseball to the Major Leagues; Reds win, 2-1.

October 8, 1939: The Reds lose the series, 4 games to 0, to the Yankees on a 10th-inning rally; Lombardi "snoozes."

October 1, 1919: The underdog Reds defeat the Chicago White Sox, 9-1, in game 1 of a tainted series.

October 7, 1961: The Yankees edge the Reds, 3-2, in game 3 of the series on a Roger Maris 9th-inning home run.

June 11, 1938: Johnny Vander Meer pitches the first of his consecutive no-hitters, against Boston.

July 31, 1935: A wild crowd of at least 35,000, many standing along the foul lines, disrupts a Reds-Cardinals night game.

June 24, 1970: The final of 4,543 regular National League games is played at Crosley Field; Reds win, 5-4.

January 27, 1937: Pitchers Lee Grissom and Gene Schott and groundskeeper Matty Schwab row a boat over Crosley's center field wall at the height of the '37 flood.

Outfield Dimensions

All outfield dimensions changed two times with park reconfigurations in 1927 and 1938, and right field alone changed four more times with the up-again, down-again "Goat Run." Dimensions are taken from architectural drawings, *The Sporting News* yearbooks, and Cincinnati Reds yearbooks.

	1912	1927	1938	1946	1951	1953	1959
LF	360	339	328	328	328	328	328
CF*	420	395	387	383	387	383	387
RF	400	377	366	342	366	342	366

*Not straight-away center field, but to deepest part of park.

Seating Capacity/Record Crowds

The seating capacity of Redland/Crosley changed significantly in 1927 and in 1939. Many other small changes in seating affected the official capacity by a few hundred seats (including the "Goat Run") but they're not included below.

1912	1927	1939	1959*
20,696	26,069	29,401	30,322

*Highest ever official seating capacity

Largest Opening Day	35,747	April 15, 1924
Largest Regular Season	36,691	April 27, 1947
Highest Season	1,125,928	1961

A Findlay & Western Timeline

1884	1895	1900	1902	1912	1927	1934
First ball park at Findlay & Western	New iron & wood grandstand built	Stands burn; club erects temporary seats	Palace of Fans opens; torn down in 1911	Redland Field opens	Field-level box seats added; fences shortened	Powel Crosley buys Reds and renames park

All-Time Crosley Field All-Star Team*

Catcher	Ernie Lombardi (1932-1941)
First Base	Ted Kluszewski (1947-1957)
Second Base	Hugh Critz (1924-1930)
Shortstop	Roy McMillan (1951-1960)
Left Field	Frank Robinson (1956-1965)
Center Field	Edd Roush (1916-1926, 1931)
Right Field	Pete Rose (1963-1970)
Right-hand Pitcher	Bucky Walters (1938-1948)
Left-hand Pitcher	Eppa Rixey (1921-1933)

Selected by fans in 1969 poll of All-Time Greatest Reds, 1869-1969

No-Hitters by Reds Pitchers at Crosley Field

Hod Eller vs. St. Louis, May 11, 1919

Johnny Vander Meer vs. Boston, June 15, 1938

Clyde Shoun vs. Boston, May 15, 1944

Ewell Blackwell vs. Boston, June 18, 1947

Jim Maloney vs. New York, June 14, 1965

Jim Maloney vs. Houston, April 30, 1969

MVP Winners in the Crosley Era

Ernie Lombardi, 1938

Bucky Walters, 1939

Frank McCormick, 1940

Frank Robinson, 1961

Johnny Bench, 1970

Rookie of the Year in the Crosley Era

Frank Robinson, 1956

Pete Rose, 1963

Tommy Helms, 1966

Johnny Bench, 1968

Crosley Field Single-Season Records

Batting Average	.353	Bubbles Hargrave	1926
Runs Batted In	141	Ted Kluszewski	1954
Home Runs	49	Ted Kluszewski	1954
Slugging Percentage	.642	Ted Kluszewski	1954
Runs Scored	134	Frank Robinson	1962
Base Hits	218	Pete Rose	1969
Stolen Bases	67	Bob Bescher	1912
Doubles	51	Frank Robinson	1962
Triples	22	Jake Daubert	1922
Earned Run Average	1.57	Fred Toney	1915
Winning Percentage	.826	Elmer Riddle (19-4)	1941
Strikeouts	265	Jim Maloney	1963
Wins	27	Dolf Luque	1923
	27	Bucky Walters	1939
Saves	35	Wayne Granger	1970

Great Performances at Crosley Field

Longest Game	21 innings, 1-0 loss to San Francisco, September 1, 1967
Home Runs in a Game	8, vs. Milwaukee (Thurman 3, Kluszewski 2, Robinson 2, Post 1), August 18, 1956
4 Home Runs in 4 At Bats	Art Shamsky, August 12 & 14, 1966
RBIs in a Game	10, Walker Cooper, July 6, 1949
Hitting for the Cycle	Harry Craft, June 8, 1940, and Frank Robinson, May 2, 1959
Most Runs in a Game	23, vs. Brooklyn, June 8, 1940, and vs. Chicago, July 6, 1949
Most Strikeouts in a Game	18, Jim Maloney (11 innings), June 14, 1965

1935	1938	1939	1946	1957	1958	1970
Light towers erected for 1st night game	Home plate moved 20 feet toward fences	Upper deck added to grandstand pavilions	"Goat Run" seating added in right field	First season for new 58-foot-high scoreboard	Last season for "Goat Run"	Final season at Findlay & Western ends June 24

Sources and Credits

Bibliography

Newspapers

Cincinnati Enquirer, Cincinnati Post, Cincinnati Times-Star, Cincinnati Commercial-Gazette, and *Dayton Daily News,* clipping files, photo files and microfilm, 1884-1990

News of the Reds, The Cincinnati Baseball Club, 1935–1952

Redleg News, The Cincinnati Baseball Club, 1953–1956

Books

Allen, Lee. *The Cincinnati Reds* (G.P. Putnam's Sons, 1948)

———. *Cooperstown Corner: Columns from The Sporting News* (Society for American Baseball Research, n.d.)

Allen, Maury. *Jackie Robinson: A Life Remembered* (Franklin Watts, 1987)

Barber, Red. *1947: When All Hell Broke Loose in Baseball* (Doubleday & Co., 1982)

———. *The Broadcasters* (Da Capo Press, 1985)

Benson, Michael. *Ballparks of North America* (McFarland & Company, Inc., 1989)

Brosnan, Jim. *The Long Season* (Harper & Brothers, 1960)

———. *Pennant Race* (Harper & Row, 1962)

Burick, Si. *Byline: Si Burick* (The Dayton Daily News, 1982)

Cincinnati Baseball Club/Cincinnati Reds (various editors). Scorebooks and Yearbooks, 1927-1971

Clark, Dick and Larry Lester (editors). *The Negro Leagues Book* (Society for American Baseball Research, 1994)

Cohen, Richard M. and David S. Neft. *The World Series* (Collier Books, Macmillan Publishing Company, 1986)

Collett, Ritter. *The Cincinnati Reds* (The Jordan-Powers Corporation, 1976)

Conner, Floyd and John Snyder. *Day by Day in Cincinnati Reds History* (Leisure Press, 1983)

Creamer, Robert. *Stengel: His Life and Times* (Simon and Schuster, 1984)

Durocher, Leo, with Ed Linn. *Nice Guys Finish Last* (Simon and Schuster, 1975)

Erardi, John. *Pete Rose: 4,192* (The Cincinnati Enquirer, Cincinnati, Ohio; 1985)

Giglierano, Geoffrey J. and Deborah A. Overmyer. *The Bicentennial Guide to Greater Cincinnati* (The Cincinnati Historical Society, 1988)

Gershman, Michael. *Diamonds: The Evolution of the Ballpark* (Houghton Mifflin, 1993)

Harmon, Pat. *Cincinnati's Greatest Sports Stories* (The Cincinnati Post, 1978)

Hertzel, Bob. *The Big Red Machine* (Prentice Hall, 1976)

Honig, Donald. *Baseball When The Grass Was Real: Baseball From The Twenties to the Forties by the Men Who Played It* (Coward, McCann & Geoghegan, Inc., 1975)

James, Bill. *The Bill James Historical Baseball Abstract* (Villard Books, 1986)

Lawson, Earl. *Cincinnati Seasons: My 34 Years with the Reds* (Diamond Communications, Inc., 1987)

Lowry, Philip J. *Green Cathedrals* (Addison-Wesley Publishing Company, 1992)

Murdock, Eugene. *Baseball Between the Wars; Memories of the Game by the Men Who Played It* (Meckler, 1992)

The National Baseball Hall of Fame and Museum, Inc., The National Baseball Library, and Gerald Astor. *The Baseball Hall of Fame 50th Anniversary Book* (Prentice Hall,1988)

Okkonen, Marc. *Baseball Uniforms of the 20th Century* (Sterling Publishing Co., Inc., 1991)

Okrent, Daniel and Harris Lewine (editors). *The Ultimate Baseball Book* (Houghton Mifflin Co.; A Hilltown Book, 1991)

Peary, Danny (editor). *We Played The Game: 65 Players Remember Baseball's Greatest Era, 1947-64* (Hyperion, 1994)

Reidenbaugh, Lowell. *Take Me Out to the Ballpark* (The Sporting News, 1983)

Ritter, Lawrence. *The Glory of Their Times: The Story of the Early Days of Baseball, Told by the Men Who Played It* (Vintage Books, 1985)

Robinson, Frank, with Al Silverman. *My Life Is Baseball* (Doubleday & Co., Inc., 1968)

——— and Barry Stainback. *Extra Innings* (McGraw-Hill Book Company, 1988)

Robinson, Jackie, as told to Alfred Duckett. *I Never Had It Made* (G.P. Putnam's Sons, 1972)

Rose, Pete and Roger Kahn. *Pete Rose: My Story* (Macmillan Publishing, 1989)

Smith, Curt. *Voices of the Game* (Fireside/Simon & Schuster, 1992)

Sokolove, Michael Y. *Hustle: The Myth, Life and Lies of Pete Rose* (Simon and Schuster, 1990)

Tiemann, Robert L. and Mark Rucker. *Nineteenth Century Stars* (Society for American Baseball Research, 1989)

Tygiel, Jules. *Baseball's Great Experiment* (Vintage Books, 1984)

Walker, Robert Harris. *Cincinnati and the Big Red Machine* (Indiana University Press, 1988)

Ward, Geoffrey C. and Ken Burns. *Baseball: An Illustrated History* (Alfred A. Knopf, 1994)

Werber, Bill. *Circling the Bases* (Copyright, Bill Werber, 1978)

Wheeler, Lonnie and John Baskin. *The Cincinnati Game* (Orange Frazier Press, 1988)

Wilber, Cynthia, J. *For the Love of the Game: Baseball Memories From the Men Who Were There* (William Morrow and Co., Inc., 1992)

Articles

The '61 Reds Oral History Project, University of Cincinnati, "From Ragamuffins to Hall-of-Famers," *The National Pastime*, No. 10.

Domanski, Robert P. "Bill McKechnie's World Champion Reds," *Bulletin of the Cincinnati Historical Society*, No. 2, 1969.

Frell, Ellen. "Waite Hoyt: The Broadcast Years in Cincinnati," *Baseball in Cincinnati: From Wooden Fences to Astroturf*, The Cincinnati Historical Society, 1988.

Meany, Tom. "Baseball Hercules," *Collier's*, May 26, 1951.

Miller, Richard and Gregory L. Rhodes. "The Life and Times of the Old Cincinnati Ballparks," *Baseball in Cincinnati: From Wooden Fences to Astroturf*, The Cincinnati Historical Society, 1988.

Miller, Richard D. "A Most Exciting and Brilliant Contest," *Timeline*, May-June, 1994.

Pietrusza, David. "The Cahill Brother's Night Baseball Experiments," *The Baseball Research Journal*, No. 23.

Shannon, Mike, "Goodbye Crosley Field–Again," *Spitball*, Jan., 1984.

Archival Materials

"Cincinnati Base Ball Club Records, 1882–1906," The Cincinnati Historical Society Manuscript Collection

"Hake Collection," The Cincinnati Historical Society Architectural Records Collection

Photo Credits

Authors

In the Crosley era, **Greg Rhodes** played shortstop for the Crosley Management Indians of Richmond, Indiana. (Powel Crosley's refrigerators and automobiles were manufactured in Richmond in the 1950s.) He attended his first major league game at Crosley Field in the mid-1950s.

Rhodes received a doctorate in education from Indiana University, has authored text books, teacher guides, and other curriculum materials, has written extensively on baseball, and is co-author with John Erardi of *The First Boys of Summer* (Road West Publishing Co., 1994). He has been a resident of Cincinnati since 1985, where he lives with his wife, Sallie, and two children, Kara and Benjamin.

Growing up in Syracuse, New York, **John Erardi** was touted as "the next Frank McCormick." The touter was Erardi's Irish mother, who as a 12-year-old girl was captivated by McCormick's glorious 1937 season for Cincinnati's top farm club of Syracuse.

Unlike McCormick, Erardi never made it to Crosley Field, but eventually made it to first base, scooping up throws for the Syracuse Moose All-Stars, Christian Brothers Academy, and later at Annapolis and Murray State University.

The *Cincinnati Enquirer* sportswriter is a graduate of Chase College of Law and author of *Pete Rose: 4192*. He resides in Crescent Springs, Kentucky with his wife, Barb, and son, Christopher.

To order additional copies of Crosley Field, *call 1-800-232-9900, or send $24.95 + $3.00 postage to: Road West Publishing, 1908 Dexter Avenue, Cincinnati, Ohio 45206.*